Thirty Years of Change Through Women's Eyes

Ireland, 1993–2023

For my big sisters,
Kay Lawler and Maura Rea,
who stayed

Thirty Years of Change Through Women's Eyes

Ireland, 1993–2023

Íde B. O'Carroll

First published in 2025 by Attic Press
Attic is an imprint of Cork University Press
Boole Library
University College Cork
College Road, Cork T12 ND89
Ireland

Authorised representative: Sinead Neville. Email: corkuniversitypress@ucc.ie

Library of Congress Control Number: 2025942548

British Library Cataloguing in Publication Data

A CIP catalogue record for this book is available from the British Library.

ISBN 9781782050803

Design and setting by Studio 10 Design
Printed by CPI in the UK

www.corkuniversitypress.com

CONTENTS

ACKNOWLEDGEMENTS

A book with such a focus on the personal could never have been written without the cooperation and trust of the women I met first in the early 1990s – many of whom have since died – and those I met again in 2023. I am deeply grateful to each of them. It is a privilege to present this final work, crafted from our encounters, to a general audience.

I wish to acknowledge those who read the manuscript at various stages and provided helpful feedback on the work: Breda Gray, Aida Keane, Margaret Lonergan and Annie G. Rogers. My friend Joan O'Brien took the photos of Margaret Galvin and Nóirín Ní Riain, in addition to driving me hither and yon in the early 1990s – *míle buíochas*. I would also like to thank visual artist Lisa O'Donnell for her beautiful cover art, entitled 'Brigid's Legacy'. Lisa created the artwork for the covers of my other two books in this trilogy, all published by Cork University Press/Attic: *Models for Movers* (1990/2015) and *Irish Transatlantics* (2018).

Gráinne Healy, feminist and friend, kindly agreed to write the foreword to this book, and no one is better equipped to do so, since she has been centrally involved in many of the social change movements and campaigns addressed in this book, in addition to leading organisations such as the National Women's Council of Ireland and the European Women's Lobby. Thank you, Gráinne.

Faculty at Trinity College Dublin's Women's Studies Centre provided vital support at a crucial time in the 1990s, for which I am deeply grateful: my thanks to Sheila Greene, Peggy Fine-Davis, Ruth Torode, Jean Whyte, Maryann Valiulis and the late Antoinette Quinn. At the University of Massachusetts-Amherst, where I taught from 2018 to 2023, I would like to acknowledge the support of Jonathan Wynn, chair, Department of Sociology, for this project.

I dedicate the book to my two big sisters, Kay Lawler and Maura Rea, in acknowledgement of their love, support and friendship.

Míle buíochas to my spouse, Annie G. Rogers, for her commitment to truth, authenticity and courage in her own writing, visual art and psychoanalytic work, which inspires me every day.

To those friends who assisted me with this project in the early 1990s – Deirdre Mortell, Mary Roddy, Teresa O'Hara and Sheila Crowley – thank you. I am also grateful to the following friends who supported my work in various ways: Martina and Denis O'Keeffe, Mary Mangan, Olivia McEvoy, Susan Coughlan, Loreto Desmond, Sheila Brown, Rena Cody, Mary Branley, Brian O'Mahony and Fiona Ryan, Elise Kaufman and Séamus Henchy, Anne Jeanne and Tom Lardner, Elizabeth Silver and Lee Badgett, Tim Goodhind, Sam Hannigan, Kathy Dunn and Colby Smith, the late Meg Turner and Pierre Johannet.

Finally, at Cork University Press I am extremely grateful to Maria O'Donovan who has been my guide through the editing process over the course of three books.

FOREWORD

This book, *Thirty Years of Change Through Women's Eyes: Ireland, 1993–2023*, is the third in a trilogy by author and social researcher Íde B. O'Carroll documenting Irish women's lives over 100 years from the 1920s to the 2020s, starting with *Models for Movers: Irish women's emigration to America* (1990/2015), followed by *Irish Transatlantics, 1980–2015* (2018), all published by Cork University Press under its Attic Press imprint. While *Models* and *Irish Transatlantics* focused on Irish women's experience of emigration and return, this book concerns the lives of women who stayed in Ireland.

Early in my professional life, I worked at Attic Press when it was a feminist press, founded by Róisín Conroy, before its purchase by Cork University Press. Therefore, I am delighted to write a foreword to a beautiful and sensitively written work.

This book reminds me, as a feminist activist involved in many of the campaigns during these decades, of the wonderful activism and feminist friendships forged during collective actions, and the hard work, determination and effort required of Irish women to ensure progress and better lives in Irish society.

Using detailed profiles crafted from two interviews conducted with each woman thirty years apart, Íde presents the lived experience of these seven women of varied backgrounds and in different places on the island of Ireland. This creates a mosaic of life for Irish women in Ireland during those three decades. The structure is effective, relatable and a clever mechanism.

Interspersed with the voices of the women themselves, Íde weaves the social and economic context in Ireland, describing the factors influencing its emergence as a modern, globalised nation state with advanced technology, massive investment, a country now considered a place of arrivals for many migrants, rather than a place of departures. Her analysis provides a backdrop to understanding women's lives and their perspectives on social change. She also offers reminders of the events that shaped women's lives and the engaged activism that led to those changes, to which many of us contributed.

A common thread in almost all the narratives, and one that touches my own life, is the importance of education in women's life journies, its contribution to the progress of women in Ireland and the progress of Irish society. My own mother was an early school leaver and believed with a passion in the value of education and pushed her seven children to get as much education as we could.

As a middle child, I was the first in my family to go to third-level education, though not the last. Education as the key to personal, social and economic progress is reflected in many of the profiles here. Also, so many of the women in this book used their education to make enormous contributions to family life, community life and Irish society, whether as editor of a magazine or a carer for children and elders, as activists and campaigners and artists.

Íde argues that the key factors influencing the collective actions and mobilisation of women in their work for social change were the growth in the number of women's groups, and women's engagement with education and EU programmes such as NOW (New Opportunities for Women) in support of women entering the labour market, managed by the NWCI (National Women's Council of Ireland). All were links in the chain strengthening and empowering women to drive towards equality and justice for all, decades of strategising, struggle, advocacy work and campaigns on reproductive rights and sexual freedoms.

In the many venues where I've honed my feminist analysis, it is the female friendships forged that keep me going. From starting with a small, community-based women's studies group called Women in Learning, to serving as chair of the National Women's Council and as a representative to various EU bodies, these friendships and the resilience of the women I have worked with have sustained and encouraged me in my work.

Of course, as is evident in the book, it was not all plain sailing. Many women suffered and continue to suffer from the failure of the state to protect women from poverty, poor health and social care, or violence against women in its ugly forms. Some of the women's profiles reflect those hard-lived lives.

Through her earlier research and publications, and here again, Íde B. O'Carroll has consistently highlighted major themes of significance in Irish women's lives. She is one of the women whose friendship and feminist collaboration I have always valued.

GRÁINNE HEALY[1]
Dublin, January 2025

INTRODUCTION

When I returned to Ireland in 1991 after studying in the USA, I was fortunate to secure a research associate position at the Centre for Women's Studies, Trinity College Dublin and to find a place to rent on Oxmantown Road in Stoneybatter, within walking distance of the city centre and a stone's throw from the Phoenix Park. I'd been drawn home by the election of President Mary Robinson in 1990 and the hope that her election generated. My plan was to begin work on a research project interviewing Irish women about their lives. The title of the project, *Irish Women and Work*, assumed that whether working inside or outside the home, for some income or none, women contributed to Irish society through their labour. The aim was to document the position of women in Irish society, in terms of the official data, but crucially, from the point of view of women. As a feminist, I wanted to foreground the words of women, to record their perspectives based on their experiences. I knew it was a valuable process because I'd successfully applied this method to a study of Irish women immigrants in the USA, *Models for Movers: Irish women's emigration to America* (Cork University Press/Attic, 1990/2015). My approach was very much influenced by the *Harvard Project on Women's Psychology and Girls' Development*,[1] and the research of Carol Gilligan and Annie G. Rogers, with whom I'd studied.

When Mary Robinson was inaugurated as president of Ireland on 3 December 1990, the first woman to hold the position, she acknowledged that she owed her success to 'mná na hÉireann / the women of Ireland'.[2] For emphasis, she included the following phrase as her understanding of the election outcome for Irish women: 'The hand that rocked the cradle, rocked the system.'

The country was in transition, moving away from the old power brokers, a move best captured in the photograph of Mary Robinson on that day: she is surrounded by a crescent of men – politicians and members of the judiciary – including a glum-looking taoiseach, Charlie Haughey, and in the background are three women: Mary O'Rourke (Fianna Fáil), Gemma Hussey (Fine Gael) and Catherine McGuinness (judiciary). President Mary Robinson declared that her aim during her term in office was to be one of 'justice, peace and love'. She spoke of how she wanted to represent a new, more open, tolerant and inclusive Ireland and extend the hand of friendship to both communities in Northern Ireland, while also recognising that the president's powers are limited by the constitution. Nonetheless, her presidency was marked by the opening of the Áras/presidential residence to its citizens and the placing of a permanently lit candle in a central window, a message to the Irish diaspora that they were not forgotten. Symbolic, yes, but powerful too. President Mary Robinson was for many women at that time, myself included, an inspiration. Her achievement and actions emboldened us.

For Irish women, Mary Robinson's election as Ireland's first woman president on 3 December 1990 represented an enormous victory because at the time, despite the work of the feminist movement in the 1970s and '80s, many Irish men still believed that a woman's place was in the home. This view is captured in an RTÉ television vox pop with Irish men on the streets, on a college campus, on a playing field, broadcast on 10 November 1990.[3] One man thinks women have no right to work outside the home and should not be considering running for president: 'It's been the way of the world for years, why should it change?' Another remarks that women should do the housework, not the men: 'It's a girl's job.' Yet another gives his assessment of Irish women's worth: 'They're only fit for kitchens, for making beds and babies.' These attitudes, expressed on the national broadcaster, the only television channel in most households, illustrate there was work to be done to ensure equality for Irish women at that time.

Between 1992 and '93 I travelled the country, visiting women living in various locations on the island of Ireland, based on recommendations from colleagues and friends and outreach to locally based women's groups. Before each visit, I posted a letter on Trinity College notepaper explaining the purpose of the study, what was involved, etc. I then followed up with those who responded, usually by letter, and if they provided a telephone number, I called to discuss their availability. In total, I met with sixty-seven women, most located outside of Dublin. I used a cassette recorder to document the descriptions of their lives and work and their views on Irish society. Several interviews were conducted *as Gaeilge*/in Irish. Many of the women were 'ordinary/extraordinary' women, only a few were public figures. To fund the project, I withdrew a small pension I'd contributed to during the seven years I spent teaching in Ireland before going to study in America. I travelled by public transport since I did not own a car. At other times, friends drove me, including Joan O'Brien who also took photos of some of the participants. People seemed to believe in the value of the project, my own mother included, her exclamation enough to encourage me: 'Isn't it high time women were asked about their lives!' Indeed.

In the summer of 2023, thirty years after our initial encounter, I met again with several participants from the original 1990s group of women comprised of those still living, contactable via regular post, and willing to meet to reflect on their experiences during those intervening decades. This time, women responded via email and provided mobile phone numbers, a measure of how far we'd come in terms of our use of technology and social networks in Ireland. These big-picture forces in society such as technology, but also economics, politics, the law and so forth, provide the context within which all lives are lived, the forces that shape and are shaped by our actions. Women participated in and witnessed major social changes in Irish society over thirty years. I wanted to hear about their experiences of change in their own lives and their perspectives on the changes in Irish society.

At the end of 1993, having depleted my financial resources to conduct the first set of interviews, I needed to focus on earning a living but always felt the desire and obligation to return to this particular project. Unfortunately, it took me many years to do so. During those intervening decades, I conducted evaluation research with women's groups, with new migrant organisations, with lesbian and gay groups, with advocacy campaigns and so forth, all relating to projects to counter inequality and social exclusion in Ireland.[4] These innovative projects were supported by several EU programmes and matching Irish government funding, in addition to private philanthropy – UK, US and home-grown Irish – which from the 1990s onwards emerged as a growing and significant source of support for the work of organisations seeking social change in Ireland.[5]

In advance of conducting the second set of interviews in 2023, I reviewed my existing data and gathered new data on the big-picture social change issues in Ireland over thirty years to inform my questions and document my observations. I provide an overview of the changing context in Chapter 1, with a particular focus on Ireland's population growth linked to a reversal of its migration trend from outward to inward migration for a period, especially from the 2000s, until emigration resumed in earnest again after the 2008 global financial crash. I also consider the rise, fall and rise again of the so-called 'Celtic Tiger' economy, discuss its impact on women generally, but in particular women's growing participation in the labour force. In addition to these changes in demographics and economics, the most remarkable structural change impacting the lives of women in Ireland has been the dramatic and unparalleled advance in legislation enabling rights for women, in a country most people outside of Ireland consider to be traditionally Catholic. I discuss the passage of legislation following referenda on divorce (1996), marriage equality (2015) and abortion (2018), against the backdrop of what I term the collapse of the Catholic Church and its moral authority because of revelations of the institutional abuse of children and women in its care. I also consider some of the challenges facing Irish women, including their underrepresentation in politics at local and national level over the decades, the escalation in violence against women, labelled as 'epidemic' by Ireland's then minister for justice Helen McEntee in 2023, and the threats posed by social media's largely unregulated misogynistic postings. Women's rights in Ireland have certainly advanced in the thirty years 1993–2023, but these gains have occurred in parallel with major risks to women's safety and well-being in Irish society.

Following a discussion of the societal context in Chapter 1, I present seven chapters in which I profile each woman's journey over thirty years comparing the fabric of their lives in the 1990s, when we first met, and its heft in 2023, highlighting the issues raised in each case.

In Chapter 2, I profile poet and writer Margaret Galvin and describe my journey to Wexford, where she lives. I notice dramatic changes to the built environment since my last visit with her thirty years ago. The massive Rose Fitzgerald Kennedy suspension bridge elegantly spans the river Barrow at the New Ross bypass. Opened in 2020, its name is a tribute to the mother of President John F. Kennedy, who visited Ireland and Wexford, his ancestral home, in 1963, just over sixty years ago. Further still, out on the N25 entrance into Wexford town, I pass a beautiful bronze sculpture of Pikemen called 'Fuascailt', meaning emancipation, erected in 1998 to commemorate the United Irishmen's rebellion in 1798. Wexford's historic past is marked on the county's landscape. Margaret Galvin describes her past, her early years in Tipperary and how those experiences shaped and influenced her work as the first woman editor of *Ireland's Own* in the 1990s, a weekly publication aimed at a traditional, rural audience and the Irish diaspora abroad. Born and raised in conditions she terms 'almost feudal', the family lived in a cottage on the grounds of a 'big house' where her father was a labourer. She understands country people and rural poverty because she's lived it. During our first meeting, she spoke of her respect for and understanding of her readers, and how she recognised the importance of the

'Lonely Hearts' section of *Ireland's Own* magazine, a measure of how life in rural Ireland offered limited opportunities to meet a partner. Thirty years later, Margaret has lived most of her life in Wexford town with her husband and an adult son with Asperger's syndrome who will require her lifelong care and support. In the intervening years, Margaret has availed of distance learning opportunities to earn primary and master's degrees via Carlow College. She's also extremely proud of the fact that she is now a published author, and a regular contributor to RTÉ Radio One's *Sunday Miscellany*.

In Chapter 3, singer and theologian Nóirín Ní Riain describes her complicated relationship with the Catholic Church, including joyful years singing with the monks at Glenstal Abbey in County Limerick where she lived for sixteen years with her former husband, musician and composer Mícheál Ó Súilleabháin and their children. Convinced from an early age that she was called to be a priest, the impossibility of such a role within the Catholic Church eventually forced her to look elsewhere. Now she's as an interfaith minister with a PhD in theology, working from her home, 'Imeall' (Edge), located outside the grounds of Glenstal Abbey. The Reverend Doctor Nóirín Ní Riain performs rituals for weddings, wakes and divorces in person and via the internet. In the vacuum created by the demise of the Catholic Church in Ireland, Nóirín believes that there is a desire among people, including 'recovering Catholics' and non-believers, for an understanding of ritual, for spiritual practice, for meaning. The Rev. Nóirín's flock is a local and a global one, made possible by her use of the internet from her little house in County Limerick. She draws on Catholic rituals that are important to her, references Sufi and Jewish traditions, and uses her fluency in the Irish language to reclaim anew the healing power of Celtic spirituality, its elemental essence, its foundation in Irish cultural practices. With her two sons, Nóirín leads groups of international visitors to engage with Ireland's ancient sacred sites and holy places in a programme they call 'Turas d'Anam/Soul Pilgrimage'. In September 2023, she began a new online adventure where she co-hosts a series of online seminars, 'Holding the Centre', for an international audience, myself included, on the topic of ageing.

In Chapter 4, I profile Garry Hynes, co-founder and artistic director of the Druid Theatre in Galway. When I first interviewed Garry in 1992 she was working as the first woman artistic director of Ireland's national theatre, the Abbey, a position she held from 1991 to '94, with some challenges along the way. Garry is now in her seventieth year, and the DruidO'Casey production of Seán O'Casey's trilogy (*The Plough and the Stars*, *The Shadow of a Gunman*, *Juno and the Paycock*) in the summer of 2023 seems like her swansong as Druid's artistic director. Tickets were snapped up by the Irish public for performances in Galway, Belfast and Dublin. I managed to experience the trilogy during its limited New York run in October. Garry Hynes' choice of work is apt. The DruidO'Casey production in 2023, just over 100 years on from the plays' conception and the establishment of the Irish nation state, is a theatrical journey that continues to be relevant, a chilling critique of modern Ireland, its national housing crisis, its massive homelessness, at a time of extraordinary national wealth. That was Garry Hynes' intention.

Living on the Aran island of Inis Mór for decades, Olwen Gill, profiled in Chapter 5, is a 'blow-in' who married a local man while still in her late teens, reared their children in the Irish language, and never left. She was running a B&B business from their home in the 1990s when we first met, responding to the island's main income source, tourism. Olwen describes her efforts to successfully educate herself since then, even from this remote location, because of the wonders of the internet. Now she works as a tour guide, explaining to 'day-trippers' arriving off the modern, million-euro ferry from Galway the significance of ancient sites like Dún Aengus, 5,000 years old, emphasising the need for preservation, protecting the island's cultural treasures and its language in the face of modernisation. She wants to see Inis Mór's community revitalised, an aim hampered by the lack of housing and strict planning regulations because of the island's designation as a special area of conservation. Her experience illustrates the complications faced by communities working to preserve their treasured past and linguistic heritage, while simultaneously making way for new homes to ensure their continued existence. Despite the recent construction of a new pier at Kilronan costing 43 million euros, Olwen describes how three local families decommissioned their fishing vessels in the summer of 2023, no longer able to make a living from the sea because of overfishing. In this most iconic of Irish tourist destinations, it's now migrant workers who staff the tourist shops at Kilronan, though they too find accommodation on the island a challenge. In 2023, housing is not just a chronic problem confined to urban areas. It is a theme that reverberates everywhere in Ireland.

When I met Ruth Mellish (a pseudonym) in 1992, she was only twenty-three. She identified as a feminist and was therefore fascinated by this project because it concerned the lived experience of women. On the day before our meeting, a bomb exploded on her route to work. That was life in Belfast then. In Chapter 6, we learn about Ruth's life in Belfast before and after the peace process, from her early work at a community centre on a state-sponsored programme to her career as an educator. Raised Presbyterian, Ruth's mother encouraged education, considered it vitally important, because her own working-class background had deprived her of that opportunity. In 2023, Ruth is an established professional, happily married to a Catholic man from the South. Her work in the field of education is with the 'digital generation', young people more accustomed to online than face-to-face exchanges. Her concerns now are with information and communications technology (ICT), its impact on learning, on people's behaviour, and the potential benefits and challenges of artificial intelligence (AI). The street violence in Belfast may be no more, but according to Ruth, threats to women there have gone underground, into the new public space of the internet, especially social media, something she has experienced first-hand, to her horror and dismay.

In Chapter 7, Patricia Hamilton discusses a juggling exercise familiar to many women who combine work for income outside the home with the bearing and rearing of children. Trained as a primary school teacher originally, she worked in that job for a few years before deciding to become a solicitor. Growing up in public housing, Patricia's parents valued education enormously, encouraged and supported their children to identify a suitable direction in life. All her siblings attended third-level education and work as professionals. When we first met in 1992, Patricia had just had her first baby. Since then, she has reared five children in rural County Clare and later in Galway city, managed her late mother's healthcare needs in Sligo, all the while working full-time, keeping going, always going, relentlessly. She speaks about the mesmerising effect of it all, the near impossibility of getting the work–life balance right, the leaning in and leaning out, years and years of it, until the death of her beloved sister forced her to re-evaluate her life and retire early, once she reached sixty.

The late Dublin-born politician Mary Banotti, the grand-niece of Irish revolutionary Michael Collins, is profiled in Chapter 8. A fighter like her esteemed relative, Mary dedicated herself to working for women's rights first at local level as a co-founder of AIM, a precursor to Women's Aid, the main organisation in Ireland working on the issue of violence against women. Elected to the European Parliament to represent the Dublin constituency, she served in this role for twenty years from 1984 to 2004, at a time when Ireland was making its case for supports to advance equality. The NOW programme – New Opportunities for Women – an initiative of the EU Commission, was the most notable programme availed of by women's groups the length and breadth of the country in the 1990s and early 2000s. Its aim was to ensure women's greater participation in the labour force. While Mary Banotti was not directly involved, its uptake and impact demonstrates the importance of Europe in terms of changes in the lives of Irish women. It was highly successful. When Mary Banotti and I met again in 2023, just over 100 years on from the establishment of the Irish state in which her famous ancestor played a part, and fifty years since Ireland joined the European Union, she was eighty-four and living in a nursing facility. She died in 2024. Her death is the only reference to an event that took place after 2023 in a book whose titled timeline is 1993–2023. In addition to the changes in social legislation impacting women's lives, to which she contributed, Mary Banotti witnessed the changing face of Ireland, with immigrants from every walk of life contributing to the growth in Ireland's diverse population. New Irish immigrants – mostly Indian, Eastern European and Filipino – were the backbone of her care team, who tended to her needs on a daily basis at the nursing home located in her home city, Dublin, a place she hardly recognised anymore because of the proliferation of apartment blocks and other dramatic changes to the built environment.

In the Conclusion I pull together the achievements of – and challenges presented by – the changes in Irish society and discuss what I consider to be some of the lessons learned from the exploration of Irish women's lives over three decades in the previous chapters. My aim here is to highlight the factors that enabled these Irish women to live full lives in their society, and what may have hindered them to do so, from my perspective.

It is important to state that all contributors bar one were given the opportunity to review the final profile I crafted from the two interviews. Ever mindful of my desire to create this work for a general audience, I have deliberately kept endnotes to a minimum, embedding references in the text as much as possible, to aid flow.

The globalisation of Ireland's economy has had major social consequences – with EU membership and massive investment by transnational corporations has come increased wealth, unprecedented inward migration and an ever-widening gap between the haves and the have-nots that endangers social cohesion. Unfortunately, this was best exemplified by the horrific and shocking street riots that erupted on 23 November 2023 on O'Connell

Street, the capital's main thoroughfare, following the brutal stabbing of children and an assistant outside Coláiste Mhuire childcare centre in the heart of Dublin city. The riots exposed a deep disenchantment in Irish society, a sentiment open to exploitation from nefarious far-right elements active on social media that seek to blame immigrants for Ireland's chronic problems – in housing and healthcare in particular – and who want to destabilise democracy and exploit divisions in society. In the context of a global shift to authoritarian rule and theocracy, action is required to counter the negative trends in society that seek to silence, subdue and return women to a more subservient role, thereby negating the positive changes.

In this book I argue that the hard-won women's rights gained over thirty years in social legislation ensuring access to divorce, abortion, marriage equality, in terms of progress towards equal pay for equal work, access to childcare supports, etc. – are a result of three factors: women's increased engagement with education; women's groups' capacity to successfully organise, advocate and campaign with allies on issues (with EU and Irish government support); and finally, the collapse in the moral authority of the Catholic Church following a succession of cover-ups of physical and sexual abuse of children and its incarceration of women in Magdalene laundries. However, I also caution that there is much work to be done since there has been a backlash to Irish women's increased presence in the workforce and by implication a shift in the traditional gender roles. The backlash is most notable in two inter-related areas: an 'epidemic' of violence against women in Ireland and attacks on women in digital public spaces like social media by anonymous actors who seek to exclude women from public discourse. This is not just a major issue for Ireland. However, it is within Ireland that most of these social media companies are located to benefit from favourable corporate tax rates. When social media companies' profit model is based on the amplification of angry and reactive posts that potentially escalate violence, endanger lives and cause division in society, in my view it raises serious questions about the need for government to intervene and ensure regulation of this crucial social space, for the good of women and for the good of society. However, it seems that the Irish state appears reluctant to bite the hand that feeds it. Ireland's wealth is directly linked to its embrace of neoliberalism – the belief in free trade, deregulation and deference to financial markets – and its attractive corporate tax rate, which has resulted in an over-reliance on transnational corporations, including global social media corporations like Twitter/X.

There are lessons to be learned from the women's lives highlighted in this book. These narratives convey the nuances and complexities of lives lived over three decades in Ireland. Since 2022 marks the one hundredth year of the foundation of the Irish state, there's an opportunity to evaluate anew the role of earlier women's organisations working for change such as Cumann na mBan, the women's arm of the Irish republican movement – their vision for an equal Irish society was never truly realised. A renewed collective action on that scale may be required to respond to the pressing challenges experienced by women in modern Ireland, many of which are local and global in nature. In conclusion, I argue that we need to recognise that as women we never truly arrive at equality – change is always necessary to improve conditions for women in society. Like democracy, equality is always a striving towards, never a given, per se. The changes required to enable a better Ireland for women from 1993 to 2023 were fought for on many levels – locally, regionally, at state level and within the European context. Through their actions at different points in their lives, the women whose narratives form the core of this book created better lives for themselves – through engagement with education, through the arts, through politics and so forth – flexible responses to a changing context. These Irish women – Margaret Galvin, Nóirín Ní Riain, Garry Hynes, Olwen Gill, Ruth Mellish, Patricia Hamilton and Mary Banotti – have demonstrated the capacity to live rich and rewarding lives often in the face of seemingly insurmountable challenges in Irish society. Social change does not just happen. Power is never relinquished voluntarily. I hope that a new generation of Irish women are inspired by these narratives and are emboldened to resist a return to the old days, to fight to retain the social changes won over these past three decades and ensure that Irish society is an even better place for women in the future.

'Hope' is the thing with feathers -
That perches in the soul -
And sings the tune without the words -
And never stops - at all -
(Emily Dickinson)

CHAPTER 1

CONTEXT – THE CHANGING ROLE OF WOMEN IN IRISH SOCIETY, 1993–2023

Those who viewed Ireland's progress from afar in 2023, the end point of this book's timeframe, may have been surprised to learn that its taoiseach/prime minister was of Irish-Indian heritage, a gay man who originally trained as a medical doctor. On the face of it, Leo Varadkar embodied change for the better in Irish society – integration of its diverse population where one in five people living on the island was born elsewhere. In 2023, the main contender for Leo Varadkar's job in a general election, should there be one, was assumed to be a woman, Mary Lou McDonald, the leader of the Sinn Féin political party, historically associated with the Irish Republican Army. She was the bookies' favourite then to be the first woman in Irish history to hold the office of taoiseach/prime minister. However, as the maxim goes, a year is a long time in politics. Perhaps a greater indicator of change in the political landscape of Ireland since 1993 was the fact that the two main political parties, Fianna Fáil and Fine Gael, who emerged from a bitter and brutal Civil War 1922–3 that followed the Irish War of Independence and the establishment of the Irish Free State, had not only successfully formed a coalition government in 2020, with the support of the Green Party and independents, but were also operating a system of rotating taoiseach/prime minister. To generations of Irish people this level of cooperation between such historical adversaries was almost unconscionable.

Against this backdrop of increased diversity and shifts in political fortunes, the number of women in Dáil Éireann, the Irish parliament, remained decidedly low: 22.5 per cent women to 77.5 per cent men in 2020. Nonetheless, in the timeframe under consideration in this book, 1993–2023, change has been afoot in Irish politics and in social legislation too, with remarkable and unparalleled advances ensuring rights for women in a country many outside of Ireland consider to be primarily Catholic: divorce (1996), marriage equality (2015) and abortion (2018) – all three notable successes that directly impact on the life choices of Irish women.

In addition, there were indicators of a thriving economy to consider. In July 2023, the government announced a budget surplus of 10 billion euros, much of it coming from low corporation tax paid by American companies in three areas - pharma, ICT and biotech. By October 2023, unemployment was at 4.8 per cent, which most economists rate as near full employment. Another economic fact, surprising to many, was that in 2022 one in eight Irish households were classified as millionaires, a factor linked to house valuations and savings according to data from the Central Bank.[1] Much of Ireland's economic success over the decades derived from its membership of the European Union, which it joined fifty years ago in 1973, and its relationship with US transnational corporations seeking a foothold in the European market via Ireland. That EU relationship in particular enabled Ireland to develop from being the poorest country in the union to being among its most wealthy in 2023, with all the consequences of a dramatic shift to a modern, globalised nation, including a concentration of its population in urban areas where the jobs are located. On the surface, in 2023 Ireland appears to be a prosperous, socially liberal and stable society. However, the riots in Dublin city centre on 23 November of that year were a shocking symptom of growing discontent at a widening wealth gap, a massive housing crisis and historic levels of homelessness – issues exploited by far-right interests to stoke anti-immigrant and anti-government anger on unregulated social media sites like Telegram. Described as 'thuggery' by an unprepared government and police force, the

Dublin riots presented a very different picture to the world than that of a prosperous and stable Irish Republic. With this overview of the good, the bad and the ugly, how did Irish society reach this point in 2023 and what were the implications for Irish women?

In this chapter I provide an overview of the main structural changes in Irish society in the thirty years from 1993 to 2023. My aim is to familiarise the reader with the big-picture changes in society, the transformative context within which the women profiled in the following chapters were leading their lives, the conditions that shaped and were shaped by the choices women made in relation to their own lives and circumstances.

I begin with a discussion of demographics and the dramatic change in Ireland's population – linked to a near reversal of Ireland's established migration pattern from outward to inward migration – leading to unprecedented diversity. I then explore the economic roller-coaster over three decades – the rise, fall and rise again of Ireland's 'Celtic Tiger' economy – and in particular the impact on women's participation in the labour market. In addition to changes in demographics and economics, I then consider the factor most impacting the rights of women in Ireland: unparalleled advances in legislation enabling divorce, marriage equality and abortion.

Demographic change: more people and more diversity

To begin, there are more people living on the island of Ireland and the demographic has never been so diverse. The population increased to 5.1 million in the Republic (2022 census) and 1.9 million in Northern Ireland (2021 census). Nonetheless, it is still below 8.5 million, the number of people living on the island of Ireland before the Great Famine of 1845. In the twelve months to the end of April 2023, the population rose by 97,600, the largest annual increase since 2008. By contrast, the birth-rate dropped by 20 per cent in the last decade, an indicator that Ireland needs migrants in its labour force and as contributors, via taxes, to its national kitty to support an ageing population – with those sixty-five and older now representing 15 per cent of the total population, based on the most recent census. Countering the perception of Ireland as primarily an agricultural nation, the majority of people live in urban areas and cities now (63 per cent), with two million people concentrated in the Greater Dublin Area according to the 2020 census.[2]

In the early 1990s, at the start of this project, emigration was still a feature of Irish life, but from the early 2000s Ireland reversed its historic migration pattern, away from outward to inward migration, so that for a period the country became primarily a place of arrivals, not departures. The numbers and places of origin of those arriving was unprecedented. Many Irish-born returning from time spent living in the UK, the US and Australia were aware, through their use of various media, that the country was on the up economically. Non-Irish people were drawn to a country perceived as economically stable, with an ageing population and a demand for labour in the services and healthcare sectors. Migrants seeking international protection, those fleeing war or climate-related events such as droughts, came in search of refuge and asylum from Afghanistan, Nigeria, Zimbabwe, Iraq and Syria.

In 2006, migrants accounted for two thirds of the increase in the population of the Republic; many were Polish and Lithuanian, influenced by the expansion of the EU by ten member states in 2004. By 2023, the country had gone from being a nation with few immigrants, about one in a hundred in the early 1990s, to a point where one in five people living in Ireland were born elsewhere. The top countries of origin now are Poland, the UK, India, Romania and Brazil. In some parts of Ireland, communities are especially diverse, like the town of Ballyhaunis, County Mayo, which has the greatest proportion of non-Irish residents at 37 per cent of the population, as reported in the 2022 census. Demonstrating the growing importance of migration, the Irish government appointed its first minister of state for integration in 2007, and its first minister of state for diaspora affairs in 2014. Following the Russian invasion of Ukraine, the Irish government offered to welcome – visa-free – and care for 100,000 Ukrainians fleeing the war. Therefore, within a short block of years, Ireland went from being relatively homogenous in the 1990s, to unprecedented diversity, with over 200 nationalities living in the Republic according to the 2016 census. There is no other country in the western world that I am aware of that has had to deal with such a dramatic migration shift in such a short period of time.

Economics: the rise, fall and rise of the 'Celtic Tiger' economy

Migration is often driven by economics. When conditions in the home country are no longer life-sustaining, people will be drawn to other countries by the prospect of work and the safety of a stable political environment. As discussed earlier, Ireland's membership of the European Union has been an important contributor to its growth and stability. The country's designation by the EU as an Objective 1 country in the 1990s deemed it a priority for EU supports, including massive structural funds which greatly enhanced the country's infrastructure, including, for example, its motorways. In addition, the EU funded and delivered designated programmes to counter social exclusion/inequality across member states. The success of the peace process in Northern Ireland (1995/1998) also offered a degree of stability and a sense of hope on the island. By 2003, Ireland's economy was thriving, the country ranked as the most globalised nation in the world because of its advanced IT, communications and financial services systems and structures.

Ireland's economic boom years from 1995 to 2007 were fuelled by the so-called 'Celtic Tiger' economy, much of it driven by multinational companies. Corporations in banking and finance chose to locate in English-speaking Dublin to establish a foothold in the European Union's market. Information technology giants like Google availed of Ireland's favourable corporation tax to establish their only base outside of the USA in Dublin, the Irish capital. Apple Computers chose to locate in Cork, along with pharma behemoths like Pfizer. The scale of US corporate presence in Ireland continued to increase into the 2000s. According to OECD statistics, the economy grew at an average annual rate of 9.4 per cent between 1995 and 2000, and between 1987 and 2007 its GDP grew by 229 per cent.[3]

When the global banking and finance crash hit in September 2008, the Irish economy went belly-up. Young people had to leave Ireland again, and in large numbers, mostly to Canada and Australia. The economic crash hit certain sectors especially hard – finance, banking, construction and property. The housing market crumbled. Unfortunately, Ireland's open economy, poor economic policies and its exposure to global markets rendered it extremely vulnerable. In addition, the Irish government's offer to bail out the banking sector and guarantee its loans collapsed the economy. As a result, Ireland lost its sovereignty to the 'Troika' – the European Central Bank, the International Monetary Fund, and the European Commission – which provided loans of 67.5 billion euro as a national bailout over three years. This bailout was on condition that the Irish government introduce austerity measures, including massive cuts to public services like housing and health, to the tune of 18 billion euros.

The Irish economy successfully bounced back after the global financial crisis, with the Irish government reporting 8 billion euro surplus in July 2023. Nonetheless, the impact of those earlier austerity measures from 2008, especially the drastic cuts in government investment in housing and healthcare, reverberates today.

Women's participation in the labour force: a growing trend

Irish women have the EU to thank for the reform of restrictive labour legislation and for programmes directly aimed at supporting women's greater participation in the labour force. The most notable reform was the removal of the 'marriage bar' in 1973, a condition of Ireland's entry to the EEC (European Economic Community, as it was then called); the 'marriage bar' decreed that women in public and state bodies had to cease working on marriage. The practice was widely followed in private enterprise and reflected the position of the Catholic Church in relation to mothers, enshrined in the Irish constitution in Article 41.2: 'The state recognises that by her life within the home, woman gives to the state a support without which the common good cannot be achieved.' It goes on to say: 'The state shall, therefore, endeavour to ensure that mothers shall not be obliged by economic necessity *to engage in labour to the neglect of their duties in the home*' (emphasis mine).

From the 1990s onwards women availed of various training and education programmes, in particular the EU's New Opportunities for Women (NOW) programme.[4] The NOW programme, to which the Irish government contributed 25 per cent of the funding, aimed to upskill women in order to support their engagement with the labour market at a time when additional workers were needed by the Irish state. The idea was that education and training was key to preparing women for jobs outside the home while also addressing issues of gender inequality in society.

The NOW programme in its various iterations was extremely significant and successful. In the 1990s, it had a major impact on building the capacity of individual women and women's groups throughout Ireland at a crucial time. The National Women's Council of Ireland (NWCI), an umbrella organisation of dozens of women's groups throughout the country, administered the NOW programme. Therefore, NWCI functioned as a central coordinating base to facilitate an exchange of ideas among women, helped to build national networks, and promoted the idea of mutual support between women's groups throughout the island, and crucially, across the EU. Each project was mandated to link with transnational EU partners in order to facilitate the exchange of knowledge and proven best practices in other member states. I researched several organisations participating in NOW. For example, a NOW project initiated by a Rape Crisis Centre involved the design and delivery of a training programme, based on European best practice, to upskill its team to respond to a major escalation in reports of sexual abuse, a critical issue in Ireland in the 1990s. Another NOW project, based in Dublin, was designed to support lesbian women and lesbian groups gain confidence, visibility and skills through bespoke training and development measures. With NOW projects empowering women in technology, women in small business, rural women, women in disadvantaged areas and so forth, the ripple effect of supporting women's greater engagement with society and the world of work for income was felt in various sectors of the Irish economy.

Throughout the 1990s and 2000s, Irish women also benefited from education at various levels, via community-based activities coordinated by organisations like AONTAS, the national adult education body, but also via third-level education, in universities and colleges. According to the Central Statistics Office (CSO), in Ireland more women now attend third-level education than men. In 2021, for example, a total of 61 per cent of all Irish adults aged 30–4 had participated in third-level education and 66 per cent were women. Irish women not only availed of education but used it to secure jobs or better jobs outside the home.

Women's increased presence in the workforce was also influenced by legislation to support them to take maternity leave without having to lose a job in order to do so. Legislation enacted in the 1990s and 2000s entitled women to maternity leave from work. The Maternity Protection Act, 1994, and later the Maternity Protection (Amendment) Act, 2004, guarantees that if a woman has sufficient social insurance contributions (PRSI), she is entitled to maternity benefit (including the self-employed) for twenty-six weeks' maternity leave. The current provision allows for an additional sixteen weeks of unpaid maternity leave. From 1975, equal pay for equal work became a legislative requirement in the public and private sectors, though it has always been difficult to monitor the concept of 'equivalence', even when a Gender Pay Gap Information Bill became law in 2018.

An interesting outcome of the economic crash in 2008 was the fact that women were drawn into the tight labour force in Ireland, and that pattern of women's growing participation rates has continued into the 2020s, well beyond the rates for men, a crucial point in terms of their access to independent income and the power that it can bestow. In 2006, for example, according to the CSO, there were 64,000 married women aged 35–9 in the labour force, a number that climbed to 75,000 in 2021. Married women in the 55–9 age bracket did even better – in 2006, 47,500 were working for income outside the home, a number that increased to 60,000 in 2021. Eurostat numbers in 2023 reveal that the average gender pay gap – the difference between what women on aggregate are paid, compared to men – is 11.3 per cent, demonstrating that Irish women still take home less pay than men, and the issue was not just confined to Ireland. Despite the fact that Irish women are more educated than men – 57 per cent of women aged 25–65 years hold third-level qualifications – they are underrepresented in the top jobs in many areas of employment.

At the heart of the issues of gender pay differentials, women's promotion prospects and their participation rates are decisions around childbearing and responsibility for childrearing. Simply put, women's work prospects and advancement are more likely than those of men to be impacted by a family's decision to have children. Women are also more likely than men to take up part-time work to facilitate childcare. In 2023, Harvard University economist Dr Claudia Golden was awarded a Nobel Prize for her work on gender pay inequality, a sure sign that this issue extends well beyond Ireland. Dr Golden's research has shown that most of the earnings difference is now between men and women *in the same jobs*, a factor that kicks in after the birth of a woman's first child. In the USA, Senator Elizabeth Warren has analysed data to demonstrate that during the COVID-19 pandemic, in heterosexual families with children, professional women remained responsible for housework and childcare. In general, men did not take up the slack, though we can assume that they saw what needed to be done and chose to ignore it. Globalised Ireland reflects global trends.

Through their labour outside and inside the home, Irish women have contributed to Ireland's successful economic recovery from the 2008 crash, a recovery that has been rapid and helped in no small measure by the revenues coming from transnational corporations concentrated in two key areas: tech and pharmaceuticals. Despite the impact of the COVID-19 pandemic from 2020 to '22 on the nation's finances, the final payment on the 'Troika' loan was made in March 2021. By July 2023, Ireland's budget surplus was estimated at 8 billion euros, the bulk of which was comprised of corporation taxes paid by multinational corporations – a blessing no doubt, but a curse should these companies choose to relocate elsewhere.

Campaigns for change and social movements

In addition to progress in terms of women's greater participation in Ireland's workforce and the benefits of an independent income, the most remarkable change impacting the lives of women in Ireland is the dramatic and unparalleled advance in legislation enabling women's rights in relation to divorce (1996), marriage equality (2015) and abortion (2018). These hard-won gains mean that Irish women have more rights today than at any other time, except perhaps under the seventh-century Brehon Laws. The legislative changes were achieved in a particular policy context, in a small society, with a population in the single digits (5.1 million in 2022), a society with significant social networking and a political culture highly attuned to constituency needs. Another contributor was the fact that the various campaigns to reform social legislation built on decades of community-based projects that facilitated a growing capacity, confidence and mobilisation of women's groups and their allies, activities that enhanced public awareness and achievement of a range of human rights issues. The campaigns organised to achieve these legislative advances were influenced by three critical success factors: the 'mushrooming' of women's groups throughout Ireland, women's engagement with education and training programmes, and diminished Catholic Church power and influence.

Beginning in the 1990s, social researcher Chris Mulvey documented a 'mushrooming' of women's groups in Ireland, based on analysis of small grants to women's groups from The Allen Lane Foundation in the UK, a trend no doubt inspired by the election of President Mary Robinson. Many of these women's groups scattered around the country also applied for European Union funding under various programmes including NOW (New Opportunities for Women), discussed earlier, aimed at mainstreaming gender equality or, in the official language of the time, to 'promote equality between men and women *in all activities and policies at all levels*' (COM (96) 67 final, emphasis mine). The NOW programme required 25 per cent of matching Irish government funds to empower women's groups to build their capacity and respond to their needs at local, regional and national levels, so the Irish state did buy-in to the programme. The National Women's Council of Ireland (NWCI) administered the NOW programme and facilitated unprecedented networking of women's groups at a national level. In 1999, building on these networks, NWCI was funded by philanthropy and the Irish government to deliver The Millennium Project, a two-year national training and development project based on a participatory learning and action (PLA) approach. The aim was to build the capacity of locally based women's groups to participate in policy formation on issues relevant to their lives. The keynote speaker at the launch of the Millennium Report in 2001 was Mary Robinson, in her capacity as United Nations high commissioner for human rights. As evaluator appointed to the Millennium Project in 2003, I reported on the effectiveness of this novel policy-related project and tracked significant successes across the key areas identified as important to those involved in the project – health, education, work, violence against women, and local development. Taking on this national policy brief was within the scope of NWCI's remit. Women's groups learned to conduct needs analysis research, prepare position papers on the key issues impacting their communities, practise delivering inputs in person at meetings of local, regional and national bodies and, crucially, to network and support one another.

Not only did Irish women learn to understand how policy formation happened but more importantly, how they might influence it, and how to get their voices heard within policy fora, work that was increasingly supported by philanthropic bodies such as The Allen Lane Foundation, UK, mentioned earlier as supportive of locally based women's groups, especially in disadvantaged areas. The Atlantic Philanthropies founded by Irish-American Chuck Feeney, a limited-life foundation, provided a vital avenue of substantial financial support to women's groups and human rights campaigns in Ireland until 2016, before its formal closure in 2020. In 2000, Community Foundation Ireland was established to promote home-grown philanthropy in Ireland, work it continues to this day. The One Foundation, founded by Deirdre Mortell and Ryanair's Declan Ryan, was another limited-life foundation like The Atlantic Philanthropies that operated from 2004 to 2014, promoting its social entrepreneur model to social change, essentially applying a business model to measures addressing social issues.

In parallel with increased support of women's groups and women's engagement with education and training from the 1990s onwards, the Catholic Church, the primary arbiter of morality in Irish society, was in freefall, inundated with scandals revealing the horrific treatment of women and children in its care. These factors contributed to the successful passage later of three important pieces of social legislation impacting the lives of Irish women following referenda on divorce (1996), marriage equality (2015) and abortion (2018).

When singer Sinéad O'Connor appeared on the US television programme *Saturday Night Live* in 1992 (3 October), after singing a rendition of the song 'War' she tore up a photograph of Pope John Paul II and pronounced the need to 'fight the real enemy'. Her intention, about which she spoke later, was to highlight the Catholic Church's institutional abuse of children in its care, including the movement of offending priests from parish to parish, knowingly exposing more children to traumatic sexual abuse. Her career as an artist suffered, as did her mental health.[5] People did not critique the pope, not then, anyway. Sinéad O'Connor was vindicated by the findings of the Commission to Inquire into Child Abuse, the 'Ryan Report', published in May 2009, which detailed horrific physical and sexual abuse of children placed by the state in the care of Catholic religious orders.[6] In 2011, Taoiseach/Prime Minister Enda Kenny, a devout Catholic, read into the record of parliament (Dáil Éireann) his summary of what had transpired – the Vatican's downplaying of what the taoiseach termed the 'rape and torture of children', to uphold its power and reputation. A few months later, Eamon Gilmore, minister for foreign affairs, closed the Irish embassy in the Vatican (3 November 2011) and recalled the ambassador because the church was simply not cooperating with the Irish government's investigation. These political actions marked an historic challenge by the Irish state to the power of the Roman Catholic Church in Ireland.

Each new set of revelations of hypocrisy and abuse of power by the Catholic Church in Ireland had consequences. In 1993, American Annie Murphy appeared on *The Late Late Show* to talk about her sexual relationship with Bishop Eamon Casey, the existence of their son Peter, an adult in his twenties, and the bishop's financial contribution towards Peter's education in the USA, funds he'd taken from the coffers of his Galway diocese. Further revelations followed about the mother and baby homes, institutions run by nuns, places where unwed mothers were sent to deliver their babies. Catherine Corless, a local historian in Tuam, County Galway, doggedly researched the mother and baby home in her town and published her findings in 2013. Her report sparked a government commission of investigation into mother and baby homes which ran from 2015 to 2017. Based on Catherine's research, some 800 infant corpses were discovered interred in a series of specially constructed chambers within an old septic tank.

The existence and operation of Magdalene laundries offered further compelling evidence of how Irish society and the Catholic Church imprisoned unwed pregnant women in Ireland over decades, up to September 1996, when the last of the laundries was closed on Seán McDermott Street in the heart of Dublin city.[7] Forced to work long hours in the laundry, the women were never paid for their labour and profits from the thriving laundry business went to the Catholic Church.

As a result of damning evidence of cruelty, corruption and the crass treatment of women and children in its care, people no longer sought moral direction from the institutional Catholic Church. Attendance at Sunday Mass plummeted. Amárach Research found that in 2023 only 14 per cent of Irish Catholics attend Sunday Mass. Therefore, in that context, Irish people took it upon themselves to be the arbiters of their own position on matters of morality – with referenda on divorce, marriage equality and later abortion all passed with the support of the majority of voters. Despite its best efforts, the Catholic Church's position in relation to these matters did not hold sway.

In this chapter I have focused on some key issues to demonstrate how Ireland has been transformed in the thirty years from 1993 to 2023, and the impact of those transformations on women's lives. Irish women now have more rights because of the availability of divorce, abortion and marriage equality and are more likely to be working for some income outside the home and are engaging with education and training in unprecedented numbers. However, they continue to earn less than men and to shoulder the main responsibility for childcare and domestic work. Nonetheless, more women in the country earning independent income signals a shift in the gender roles in society.

Unsettling established gender roles can have consequences and can spur a backlash. A referendum to change the Irish constitution's Article 41.2, discussed earlier, and its reference to women's 'duties in the home' that should have taken place in November 2023 was postponed. Despite major advances for women in Ireland, incidents of violence against women, including violent deaths, have reached 'epidemic' levels according to then justice minister Helen McEntee, requiring a new domestic, sexual and gender-based violence (DSGBV) government agency, announced in September 2023. In a profile in *The Irish Times* on 18 November 2023, former state pathologist Marie Cassidy explained that women are far more likely to be killed by someone they know than by a stranger: 'It's the man in your bed not under your bed that you should be worried about.'

Like democracy, equality for women is always a striving towards, one change at a time, never a point of arrival, per se. In 2023, the endpoint of this book, in the context of a global shift to authoritarian rule and theocracy, the most pressing threat to women in Irish society is in the largely unregulated digital sphere, the virtual, online world of the internet and its various platforms. Algorithms are used to amplify posts that spew hate and disinformation, promote chaos and uncertainty. The business model thrives on the promotion of misinformation and disinformation that fuels division and increases traffic thereby boosting profits and dissolving decades of work to achieve equality in society.[8] In this digital public space, social media companies such as Facebook and Twitter/X, owned by men, are acting like cowboys in the old Wild West, behaving as they wish, with not a sheriff in sight. When Elon Musk acquired Twitter in 2022 for 44 billion dollars one of his first acts was to dispense with its DEI staff – diversity, equality and inclusion. With each new shift in technology – the internet and social media – the threat to women is real, not imaginary, in this new public space of society. Pornography that degrades women is widely available to users of all ages via the internet. Misogynistic exchanges are posted by anonymous players and bots on multiple social media platforms. Legacy media – newspapers, television, radio – while seemingly still trusted in Ireland, are no longer the first sources consulted by the majority of people for news. This is not just an Irish issue, but a global one, demonstrating that the globalisation of Ireland's economy has had major social consequences.

Conversely, the internet has also been a major force for positive change in the lives of Irish women, enabling access to education, facilitating information exchange, fuelling campaigns for change and supporting personal, professional and community development. The experience of several women in the following chapters provides evidence of the internet's positive impact. For example, Nóirín Ní Riain, Margaret Galvin and Olwen Gill all gained advanced degrees via remote or hybrid models of education, and Garry Hynes used the internet to broadcast Druid's theatrical productions during COVID, thereby maintaining connection with its loyal audience in addition to gaining new followers. Their experiences suggest that it is how society manages technological change that is at issue, not the advances themselves.

Despite the major economic and social progress for women outlined in this chapter, glaring inequalities remain in terms of housing, homelessness, healthcare, and a disturbing, growing epidemic of violence against women.

Many of the issues outlined in this context chapter arise also in the profiles of the women that follow. For example, in Chapter 2, Margaret Galvin discusses rural poverty and her work as a writer who also supports a neurodivergent son whom she must parent for life. In Chapter 3, Nóirín Ní Riain describes her move away from the Catholic Church and how the internet has facilitated her ability to respond to people's 'hunger' for spirituality. Theatre director Garry Hynes discusses the housing crisis in the context of the DruidO'Casey trilogy in Chapter 4, while Olwen Gill raises her concerns about housing and community life on an Aran island in Chapter 5. In Chapter 6, Ruth Mellish relates her successful work as an educator, but also her experience of online abuse and harassment of women which not only undermines women's rights, but also democracy at large. Patricia Hamilton provides a clear account of the juggling required to be a mother of five children and a professional solicitor in Chapter 7. Finally, in Chapter 8, former politician Mary Banotti speaks of the importance of women's engagement with politics and the positive contribution of Ireland's new migrant population to society.

CHAPTER 2

MARGARET GALVIN

Margaret Galvin describes growing up in an era of 'serfdom' in 1950s Ireland because of her father's job as a farm hand on the estate of Lieutenant Colonel Charteris (1866–1961), in Cahir, County Tipperary, a prosperous town in the heart of the fertile Golden Vale, dominated by the river Suir. According to records held at the University of Galway, in the 1870s the Cahir estate was comprised of 16,616 acres. During Margaret's childhood, the demesne was owned by what she describes as 'the bastions of the landed gentry of south Tipperary'. Her father's position entitled him to the use of a cottage on the estate, and a meagre income. However, once he was diagnosed with 'rheumatic fever leading to a heart condition' early in the life of his young family, their hardship intensified as they 'scrambled' to survive as best they could on very little. At our first meeting in 1992, Margaret explained that her mother, when Margaret was born, was forty-eight years old. Margaret was the last of five children, with a gap of nine years between herself and her next sibling.

> My father was confined to bed with it [rheumatic fever], which he contracted as a young man working on the estate. The poignant significance of the whole thing only really came through to me in the last three years, through Gestalt therapy – connecting with my mother's terror, medical fear, social fear, the grinding horror of poverty.

Margaret Galvin, 1992
PHOTO BY JOAN O'BRIEN

Growing up in the context of the 'big house' informed Margaret's inquiring mind, spurred her desire to understand how a feudal system impacted the daily lives of labourers, shepherds and dairymaids, people who were her neighbours, all living in twentieth-century Ireland under conditions established in another century. It was only in 1885, under the terms of the Ashbourne Land Act, that the main function of the Irish Land Commission (established in 1881) was transformed from ensuring fair rents for tenants to breaking up existing big estates. Between 1885 and 1920, the commission oversaw the transfer of over 13 million acres of land, which gives us a sense of the extent of such estates, Ireland's colonial legacy. After Irish independence, the commission continued to acquire land and distribute it, often to former tenants, though Margaret's family was not part of this process because her father was a farm hand, not a tenant.

Margaret has never forgotten her origins under this system, the deep poverty endured by ordinary people, her neighbours, how her family learned to make do with the bare minimum.

Her mother reserved 'two good cups' for special visitors, because hospitality and connection were vital under such circumstances. Despite their limited resources, Margaret remembers that they shared what they had with their neighbours, and their neighbours shared with them.

Ever observant, her experience and early understanding of social class differences influenced Margaret, her life decisions, and her ability as a young woman to deal with a shifting social context. Education was the route to her own social mobility, to rise up from the 'serfdom of my parents'. At the local primary and secondary schools in Cahir, she was 'passionately aware … of the implication of the 1967 Education Act [free secondary education] because for the first time, the option of third-level education was there in theory for the likes of me, but it was theoretical'. Her mother encouraged her. Her father was less inclined to do so. His advice: 'Would you not go to the tech and do a secretarial course?' He was, she remembers, advocating the safe path, 'out of his own fear'.

Margaret's decision to pursue a degree at university was both 'exhilarating' and daunting. She knew there 'was something frightening, glorious … opening up' for her. Only one other person in her family had completed secondary school. Determined to give it her all, she attended University College Cork (UCC) to study sociology and English. She found the social context challenging, given her background, and she tried to adjust to the 'middle-class values' that she felt dominated all aspects of life on campus. Navigating this alien territory was a very lonely and isolating experience and she left university at the end of her second year.

She felt confused and discombobulated. 'What in the name of God am I doing here?' There were support systems at UCC, but Margaret 'always felt that I was very removed. They couldn't accommodate me because they [support services] were all peopled by middle-class [staff], functioning at such a social remove from me and such an emotional remove from me that I would only further reinforce my own very sharp isolation by ever looking for help.'

Even though she was young, she had a mature perspective on her situation: it was not only the university system that failed her, as she saw it, but 'my own hang-ups and inabilities' and fear. After leaving UCC, Margaret moved with a partner to Wexford where she found a job at the local library and remained working there for ten years.

When we first met in September 1992, Margaret was living in Wexford town, working at a job she loved as an editorial assistant and later the first woman editor of *Ireland's Own*, in existence since 1902, a weekly publication aimed mostly at rural people and members of the Irish diaspora. The publication, originally a family business, was owned then by Independent Newspapers and had a circulation of 52,000. Her capacity to appreciate and claim her background as 'rural poor' is what prepared her for the job, especially its 'Lonely Hearts' column, much in demand by the readership, as indicated by the volume of letters received – up to 900 a week – in response to notices posted. 'We're dealing with … the human dilemma, presented to you in a very raw and very trusting state.' The popularity of the magazine with its core audience – rural, conservative, Catholic – seems at odds with people's conception of Ireland in the 1990s, a time when most of the country's population was concentrated in Dublin city.

> You're dealing with a unique and very unpretentious section of the community. I'm very aware of the sensitivities, deep refinement of sensibilities required in dealing with the readership of the magazine. It may be perceived as very traditional in outlook, but we certainly don't compromise on quality. You might find a short story by James Joyce alongside some come-all-ye of a song. The co-existence of the two is something I celebrate in my own nature. It is very Irish. There is no snobbish demarcation on what is acceptable. The nature of the readership lends itself very much to accommodate that degree of quirkiness.

Margaret explained that the very loyal readers of *Ireland's Own* were people who shared a desire for stories that reflected a depiction of their lives and concerns, traditions of the past remembered in a modern and modernising nation. Margaret understood and respected her readers. During her tenure, she made a point of presenting the work of women writers like Maura Laverty to her audience because the subject matter dealt with the experiences of rural women. Margaret's work with *Ireland's Own* was far more layered, significant and powerful than I'd first imagined and seemed like a window onto a different Ireland.

In addition to editing *Ireland's Own*, she was writing fiction and poetry, often with this same audience in mind, recalling her experiences of times past in stories, poems and prose, writing that mirrored a hidden Ireland – poor, rural, Catholic, connected and yet lonely too. Margaret did not gloss over the hardship, the cruelty, the social class evils that played out daily in ways that people understood but seemed unable to accept or change. There was the man once told by a teacher that he was a fool, an incantation he'd carried all his life. He relayed the story to Margaret in his late sixties with such a force of outrage in his voice that it was as if the insult had only been delivered the day before.

> Writing comes in waves. If you're not writing for a while, it goes from you. You have to discipline yourself. It's the small old half bit of a half-said thing that's often a much more powerful way in … It's subtle.

Her early short stories were published by the legendary David Marcus' *New Irish Writing*, carried in the *Irish Press* newspaper. Her first collection of poems, *Miresuck and Slaver*, was produced by Tuba Press, London in 1989. It was written in the period 1987–9, shortly after the ending of a long-term relationship. The second collection, *Habitual Keeper*, was due out in early 1993, a few months after our first meeting in Wexford. She sees it as a very important work.

> It comprises eighty-five poems written over a painful period [when I was in therapy]. I had been fortunate enough to have been able to afford … therapy. It was then I connected with my childhood … It was then all that came home to roost.

Her work at *Ireland's Own* kept her going, as did Margaret's connection to the Wexford community: 'With them, I can say this is how it was and we're celebrating [the publication of the poetry collection, *Habitual Keeper*]. My spirit is lively, and I want the luxury of being able to pick up the glorious, eclectic every day.' She found the discipline of a writing life challenging in the 1990s because she worked five days a week at the magazine, but Margaret was pleased with her life, determined to work hard: 'I love Wexford. I love being a provincial woman – finding the infinite in the everyday, in a delightful marriage of what transcends and what is colloquial.'

In the intervening years, before our second meeting in 2023, I'd heard Margaret's writing broadcast regularly on *Sunday Miscellany*, a popular Sunday programme on the national radio station, RTÉ. As a result, I was aware that she had continued with her craft in the thirty years since we last met in 1992 when she'd been a young woman of thirty-three. When we meet again in June 2023, she's sixty-four years old.

As I drive to Wexford town on a glorious summer's day in June 2023, I pass a beautiful sculpture of the Croppy Boys, the United Irishmen rebels, with their pikes held high, a reminder of local courage during the 1798 rebellion against British rule. Wexford now boasts the longest suspension bridge in Ireland, the Rose Kennedy Fitzgerald. In these public monuments located on either side of a thriving town, the past and present blend and seem to mirror a key theme in Margaret's creative work. The core of Wexford town weaves inwards and upwards from the water's edge, its quayside now dominated by modern hotels, brightly coloured shopfronts, apartment blocks. I drive up a warren of ancient, narrow streets, past medieval buildings, rising to mid-twentieth-century housing estates overlooking the town. I pull up to the home Margaret and her husband Philip bought in 1995.

Once we're settled with tea, Margaret tells me that in addition to her marriage to Philip, the other main change in her life was the birth of their child, Ibar, twenty-five years ago. Born three months premature and weighing a little over a pound, Ibar had to deal with major health issues. Therefore, care work became the family's focus. Her husband, a teacher, stayed home at first and later availed of a career break to allow Margaret to continue her work at *Ireland's Own*, but in time her job had to go.

> I'll never forget going in to hand in my notice at work. I didn't begrudge at all taking on the caring role, but I was certainly terrified by the implications of that role, of being responsible for such a fragile human being … It was surreal, in retrospect. There was nothing else in our lives. We were in Crumlin hospital … and the local hospital every second day.

The medical prognosis from the doctors was summarised in just one word – 'never' – casting doubt over the child's capacity to ever attend mainstream school.

> We had to hold on to the fact that even though you're driving home with that [word 'never'] ringing in your ears, the child you're with now is the same child you brought up in the car this morning, before the 'never' was hurled at you. We were very determined, in a realistic kind of way … So, our son did go to mainstream school. He did his Leaving Cert. His over-riding diagnosis now is … Asperger's.

With her son's health and development as the family's priority, Margaret was grateful to live in Wexford where by pure chance, or what she calls 'postcode lottery', the state's health board provides a day service for people with autism/Asperger's syndrome called

KITE. Ibar now attends KITE three days a week. Margaret counts her blessings, knowing that families living in other counties are not so fortunate. There's a crisis in social care in Ireland, she explains, a combination of staff shortages, overstretched services, and stringent rules and regulations. However, organisations such as AsIAm, for example, have contributed to the growing awareness of autism in Ireland and the needs of people on the neurodivergent spectrum. It's a topic Margaret returns to often but she wants to also tell me about the joy she has experienced with her family.

She married in 1996, a few years after we first met in Wexford. Her husband, Philip, had been a priest, principal of the local secondary school, someone she had met at cultural events, plays and concerts over the years. His family background was working class, so they have a shared understanding of the nuances of such an upbringing, the contradictions – the sense of lack and the inherent richness too. I am curious to know if their marriage created a controversy in the town. Margaret tells me that was not the case because Philip was highly regarded as 'a really decent human being who had a fantastic history as a teacher, loved by his pupils, and terribly decent'.

As Ibar's progress became their focus, they decided it made more sense ultimately for Philip to continue in his teaching job, which paid well and offered long holidays. Therefore, Margaret had to give up her work at *Ireland's Own*. It was not an easy decision for her – she 'cried every day for three months'. She recalls seeking counselling and being advised that in order to cope, she had to 'roll up the sleeves' because she was in for the long haul. Essentially, she and Philip would be parenting for life. As a result, she became a passionate advocate for educational supports for children with different learning needs. During what she describes as 'seven lean years', when her beloved son's health issues required her full attention, she was simply unable to concentrate on writing. She only returned to writing once he started attending mainstream school.

Back in the writing groove, her creative output was in flow. She won the Brendan Kennelly Award in 2005, which led to the publication of a collection of poems called *The Waiting Room* – a significant turning point for her. She also attended courses offered at the local library in storytelling, organised by the University of Glanmorganshire. Out of this experience emerged a book of what she describes as 'narrative poem stories' entitled *The Wishbone* and later she published *The Wardrobe Mistress*. Her 2013 publication *The Scattering Lawns* concerns the theme of emigration. It's a collection close to her heart because all of Margaret's family had to emigrate to England. She explains how her siblings, who were much older than her, did not benefit from the availability of free secondary school education, which was only introduced in 1967. Therefore, they had to emigrate at a young age, to seek opportunity across the water, with only minimal education. None of them returned.

> My family all emigrated to England. Chronology was hugely on my side in terms of being educated. My brother became a painter and decorator in England, in Dulwich … He died very suddenly of a brain haemorrhage, only in his sixties. The 'scattering lawns' of the title refers to the area around a crematorium for scattering ashes. It was a very peculiar experience going over to bury him, someone I hadn't seen for decades.

In 2019, Margaret was commissioned by the Historical Society in Cahir, her place of birth, to write a series of poems about growing up there in the 1960s and '70s – the result is entitled *The Finer Points*. At our meeting in June 2023, she gives me a copy of her latest work, to be launched in Wexford and Cahir, a collection of poems and prose pieces, *Our House, Delirious*, most of which Margaret presented on RTÉ's *Sunday Miscellany* over the years. Its title refers to the high jinks and fun generated when her brother, the painter/decorator in England, on one of his rare visits to the family home in Cahir, brought home a record player as a gift, at a time when the dancehall scene in Ireland was thriving. The collection is full of humour, honesty and compassion.

> It's a collection of prose and poetry, divided into four sections. The first section deals with men, the dilemmas of men, as I saw and understood them. The second is the dilemmas of women. Then a biographical, memoir section. The final section is quite hilarious, built around Babycham, Brendan Bowyer and the dancehalls. Our next-door neighbour in Cahir was the caretaker of the Arcadia Ballroom. He'd be telling me about the bands – The Dixies, Ray Lynam and The Hillbillies, Dickie Rock. It was the period of the dancehalls.

When I ask about other changes she's witnessed in the thirty years since our first meeting, she turns her attention to observations about the Catholic Church, adamant of the need to distinguish between the role of the institution and her experience of well-intentioned people within it.

> There's been an enormous erosion in credibility. There's the institution and this ferocious litany of human rights abuses. Look at the Ryan Report. The Ferns Report. The Cloyne Report. The Dublin Report. The Industrial Schools. The Magdalene laundries. And Tuam. Mother of God, is it ever going to end? You had it in the posh schools, Blackrock and Templeogue, middle-class men, men in their sixties, professional people. It wasn't just the poor [who were abused]. The litany of human rights abuses has certainly taken its toll – why wouldn't they?

She's aware of the diminishing presence and power of the Catholic Church in Ireland in 2023. To illustrate her point, she explains how a child asked her recently what a nun was, because the child had never seen one. She then describes a funeral she attended of a very old man, a professional, a devout Catholic, educated by religious, and how she observed that those attending – 'the old, well-off people', deeply committed to their faith – represented the last of their kind. From her point of view, the credibility of the institution has been 'severely eroded', and the main prospect for a new lease of life lies with some of Ireland's immigrant population, people from places that were formerly the focal point of Irish Catholic missionaries – places like the Philippines and India. She also acknowledges that people who are not practising Catholics still engage in major religious rites like weddings and funerals in churches, so perhaps a new alternative model may evolve in time.

Immigrants have sought a new life in Wexford, as in many parts of Ireland, during the years spanning the focus of this book, 1993–2023. However, in 2001 tragedy struck in Wexford when six men and two boys, believed to be refugees, were found dead in a container in Rosslare port, close to Wexford town; another four men and a woman were barely alive. This was the first such tragedy in Ireland and illustrated the desperate measures migrants were willing to take in order to reach the country. In 2023, the nearest direct provision centre for asylum seekers in Wexford is located by the ocean at the old Courtown Hotel where 230 international protection applicants (IPAs) await processing by the government. Eastern European migrants – Polish, Latvians and Lithuanians – arrived in Wexford from 2004, after the EU expanded its membership. In her role as a volunteer English language teacher, Margaret has direct experience with migrants in her town.

> The Polish were a great novelty to us altogether even though they were White and Catholic. They reminded us of what we were in the 1950s – [they] worked three jobs, for nothing. A good number of Syrian people [now]. They keep very much to themselves. No direct provision centre yet [in Wexford town]. The local garda station [disused] and a big destination hotel up the road have just been purchased by private companies [for future use as direct provision centres].

Her experience of working with migrants from Eastern Europe and later with IPAs from Syria has provided some degree of perspective on the enormity of the process of change in Ireland's cities, towns and villages. From Margaret's point of view, the extent of the cultural divide was significant, with little being done to explain the cultural norms of migrants and the social norms of Wexford people, a two-way process of learning about and understanding differences, a process she sees as crucial to any form of successful integration in Ireland.

> I was [helping with] a homework group for small children as a volunteer. I found it difficult when the men [from Syria] would come in to collect the children and would make a lavish display of shaking his [young male manager's] hand and being very grateful to him – as if I didn't exist. With the best will in the world, of trying to understand, of trying to bring cultural competence to bear, I found myself annoyed. I did feel that cultural competence cuts two ways. I wonder about acculturation training, knowledge and information … say hello to the locals. It would really help. It may be difficult to make eye contact, if you're a woman. Proper integration, not a token thing with people finding their feet, [requires] they can link with all sorts of community organisations. The government will have to wake up to the fact that you cannot bring busloads of foreign nationals into a town at three o'clock in the morning. What message is that sending? This is clandestine. This is dangerous.

The faces she encounters on the streets of Wexford represent modern Ireland – diverse, multicultural and multiethnic. In the past, she explains, the community would have looked to the Catholic Church for guidance in terms of such dramatic change in the composition of communities and society. Indeed, various churches and faiths appear to be responding to the needs of new communities of different faiths – Catholic, Protestant, Muslim, Hindu, etc. However, in terms of social change, Margaret believes that the results of recent referenda in relation to divorce, marriage equality and abortion demonstrate that 'the days are gone' when the Catholic Church will dictate to the people. People seeking understanding are guided by public figures and by their own moral compass. To illustrate her point, she cites the marriage equality campaign and the intervention of people like singer Daniel O'Donnell whom she heard on the radio declare: '[Majella and I] are very happy and why wouldn't we want other people to be happy?' His reassurance that 'this doesn't diminish my happiness as … a married man one iota' drove home the point, in Margaret's view. And she also discusses the input to the campaign by sports people such as Babs Keating of Tipperary GAA, and the late historian and nun, Margaret MacCurtain.

In addition to the successful passage of marriage equality, passed by 62 per cent of voters, within the timeframe of this book, 1993–2023, results from other referenda are indicative of a radically changed Ireland, a growing liberal consensus and generational shift. The referendum on divorce in 1995 passed with a slim majority of 50.28 per cent, and was signed into law in 1996. The 2019 referendum to ease restrictions on divorce was passed by an overwhelming majority, 82.01 per cent. The referendum in 2018 to overturn the abortion ban passed with 66.4 per cent in favour.

Besides the introduction of social legislation, another key feature of change since Margaret and I last met is the ubiquitous nature of information and communications technology (ICT), the use of email, internet and mobile phones. She's availed of supports in her local library to navigate these changes, learning how to use a computer and email in her work. During COVID, she transitioned to the use of Zoom, a forum that cut across her isolation and enabled her to stay connected to community. ICT also facilitated her own continuing education and development. A lifelong learner, Margaret is very proud of her creative output, something she links to her own evolving sense of herself, her family and, most of all, her growing confidence. She is also extremely proud of the fact that she not only completed but excelled in studies for undergraduate and master's degrees through Carlow College, courses offered via the college's satellite base in Wexford. She completed both degrees, with distinction, by the time she was fifty-six, achieving 'Student of the Year' awards at each graduation.

> I went in 2009 to do a four-year degree [Social Studies], then a two year master's. It was a really reflective time for me. Social Studies was fascinating and psychology – Erikson's lifespan theory, the age categories … Of course, they'd be different now because of life expectancy. The one that really stuck with me was generativity versus stagnation, a verification of my own life journey, amplified in my exploration of others' lives. A change I would praise to the hilt is lifelong learning, serious adult education. I did my thesis on people who do their first primary degree past the age of forty.

With her degrees successfully secured, Margaret began to teach courses in creative writing. In 2023, she was teaching such courses part-time, mainly in what she calls a 'social care setting'. She delivered a recent course for elders along with local playwright Billy Roche, a scheme supported by a number of bodies, including Poetry Ireland, called 'Songlines'. She also facilitates writing for people with intellectual disabilities, work supported by the Health Service Executive.

While writing and teaching are once more important aspects of Margaret's life, she becomes most animated when talking about her son Ibar, her 'duty of care' to him, which is a constant in her life, a responsibility that 'extends to connecting into every organisation'. She works diligently to ensure that there will be sufficient supports in place for him once she and Philip are gone. 'You do have a consciousness of mortality', a need to try and ensure that 'they [health services] can provide for our son', who has support needs. It's advocacy work she's done for decades to ensure that her son has the support he needs to live a full and rich life. His condition, Asperger's, is a form of neurodiversity that can impact his capacity to live, work and interact socially. However, as she and Philip age – she's sixty-four and Philip seventy-three – she's focused on Ibar's future because of the 'patchwork of support services' for adults with neurodivergent needs. Nonetheless, she's grateful for all that she has in her life now.

> I don't mind being the age I am. I've had a very rich and varied life, even with the extremes handed to me, growing up poor, now being very comfortable. We choose a very modest lifestyle. We have the resources to do more if we so wished. There's a great freedom and security and dignity that attaches to that. We're kinder. The country is kinder. We have to live and let live. Are we the only people who deserve water in the tap, electricity from the grid, [access] to library books and a school? People shouting at poor old divils that have come from God knows where, economic migrants ... Everyone belonging to me was an economic migrant. Who do we think we are? We forget very quickly, don't we?

Margaret Galvin, 2023
PHOTO BY THE AUTHOR

On my way out of Wexford town, I see several Southeast Asian people walking the streets, going about their business on a fine summer's day. As I pass a local primary school, among the children set loose from their studies I notice several Black children making their way home at the end of the school day. The transformation in Wexford town's population is clearly visible, everywhere. The test of time will be how well the integration process is managed by the community. The government agencies and NGOs involved in this crucial process would do well to consult Margaret Galvin, given her vast experience as an astute observer, an outsider initially who managed to become an insider deeply engaged with her community.

CHAPTER 3

NÓIRÍN NÍ RIAIN

'Tis a gift to be simple, 'tis a gift to be free,
'Tis a gift to come down where we ought to be,
And when we find ourselves in the place just right,
'Twill be in the valley of love and delight.

'Simple Gifts', a traditional Shaker song from the eighteenth century

I was familiar with Nóirín Ní Riain's work as a singer in the traditional Irish style before I first met her in Boston in March 1991, when she agreed, without hesitation, to be part of an 'Irish Women in Boston' conference. She brought to that women's gathering the magic of her singing – in Irish and English – her warmth, her healing energy, her generosity of spirit and the joy of her stories, told in a strong east Limerick accent. Nóirín opened her contribution by singing 'Simple Gifts', a traditional Shaker song. Then she engaged us in ritual – the lighting of candles and the recitation of incantations to bless the gathering – ceremonial rites that reflected an Ireland several centuries old and, from our location, some 3,000 miles away. Her parting gift on that day was a commitment to ensure that those attending the conference got invited to Irish events at Boston College, the Jesuit institution, where her husband, composer and musician Mícheál Ó Súilleabháin, was a visiting scholar for the year.

On my return to Ireland, I wrote to Nóirín about this project on Irish women and explained my desire to include her narrative. Ever generous, she met me in September 1992 in a hotel in Temple Bar, Dublin, which was then a shabby and even dodgy area before its development really took off. At that time, she described her relationship with singing as 'a compensation and a consolation'. Her life to that point (she was forty-one years old) had been marked by periods of what she described as 'trauma and transformation', connected to her art form and her relationships. Nonetheless, she assured me that, during the highs and the lows, what anchored her, always, was a strong faith in God, 'who'll look after me'.

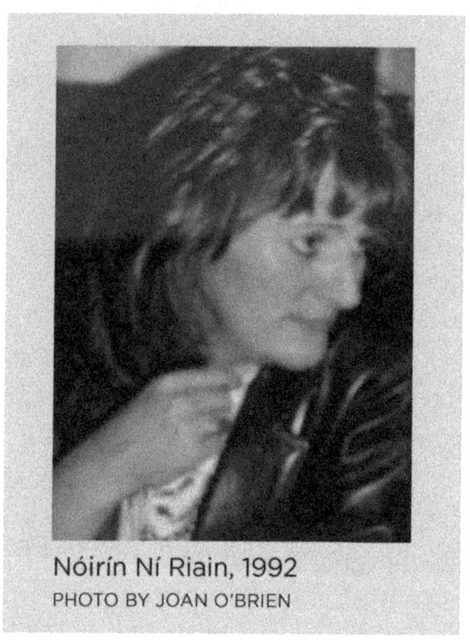

Nóirín Ní Riain, 1992
PHOTO BY JOAN O'BRIEN

A devout, practising Catholic then, she, Mícheál and their two children were living on the grounds of Glenstal Abbey, a Benedictine monastery in County Limerick, a base that facilitated her daily observance of the monks' offices, though as a woman she could never participate fully in their religious ceremonies, something she longed to do. As a young child, each Sunday Nóirín 'said Mass' in her parents' bedroom, by the fireplace, dispensing Silvermints (Irish sweets) as Holy Communion to imaginary parishioners. Even though it was joyful play that comforted a child's imagination, she thought of it as a preparation for her true role in life. When her brother caught her in this mode one day he laughed heartily and told his young sister that she could never be a priest. Never! Little Nóirín was crestfallen. She learned very quickly the rules of the Catholic Church – that women could not conduct church rituals and, crucially, were excluded from becoming priests, and by extension bishops or cardinals or pope. True power resided with the men of the cloth in the Roman Catholic Church. However, the desire to become a priest never left Nóirín. She would find a way.

Born and raised by Lough Gur and its stone circle at Grange, County Limerick, a Neolithic site 5,000 years old, Nóirín has always had a sense of the Other World/Áit Eile close by. The physical landscape of her birthplace is marked by monuments to greater forces beyond this world, places of sacred, communal, ritualistic gathering. When her head touched the centre stone in the circle at Grange she felt 'a powerful surge of energy and heat'.

Her parents had always encouraged her singing, particularly her father. They arranged for her to have singing lessons with Mary McDonagh in Limerick, starting when she was seven years of age. During the next five years, singing became a focus of her life as she developed her talent, winning singing competitions in the under-17 category when she was only eleven years of age. During her teenage years at boarding school, Nóirín was singled out by the nuns for her wonderful singing voice, which isolated her from her peers, not a pleasant experience for any adolescent.

> It was totally different [at boarding school in Dundalk]. [It was] like going to another country. I hated it. I remember being very lonely. For the first three years it was terrible. I went to Dundalk as a singer, so anytime there would be visitors, bishops and the like, they'd push me up on the stage. I didn't object for two years.

At age fourteen, one incident dramatically impacted her capacity to perform as a singer in public. Cast as the lead role in that year's school operetta, Gilbert and Sullivan's *Iolanthe*, Nóirín went on stage without her wings on the night when an important local patron of the school, Tyrone Guthrie, was present in the audience. 'I came off the stage and a nun hit me vehemently across the face. She was very upset because it [absence of the wings] might have ruined [the operetta].' The act was so violent that from 'then until the age of thirty-six, I couldn't sing in public'. Nóirín objects to my naming the nun's physical blow as an act of violence and chooses to interpret it as a 'lack of confidence in me'. In addition, the nun had communicated a cruel message: 'You [Nóirín] could never do anything right.' For the talented adolescent, everything was shifting, including at home, where all was not well with her parents' relationship, a dynamic she could not change, much as she might like to. 'It was a very traumatic time … my nerves, and the changes.'

However, another person entered her life, someone new to believe in her and her singing abilities. Pilib Ó Laoghaire from UCC's Music Department came to her school to examine Nóirín for her Leaving Certificate music exam. After their encounter, he asked her about her career plans, since this was her last year in secondary school. When she responded that she was planning to study law, Pilib responded, 'You're not. You're coming down to do music at UCC.' Nóirín was delighted with his confidence in her: 'It was just brilliant. I wasn't making a decision myself.' He had total confidence in her talent.

Therefore, during her formative years, Nóirín had two important mentors – her singing teacher Mary McDonagh in Limerick, followed by Pilib Ó Laoghaire at UCC.

> The two things that would always be lacking for women in the arts [in Ireland] would have been patronage and education. I was blessed with both. Both mentoring relationships were very intense. He [Pilib Ó Laoghaire] tutored me in over 200 songs he'd collected over the years, Déise songs [from the Waterford Gaeltacht].

At University College Cork she met her future husband, Mícheál, who was also a music student. They both fell under the spell of the legendary composer and professor Seán Ó Riada.

> My first day in college, I met Michael Sullivan at the top of the stairs. Ó Riada was full of everything Irish [the language, the music]. He imbued his students with it [a deep love of Irish culture].

Consequently, Nóirín and Mícheál changed to the Irish version of their names – Ní Riain/Ryan and Ó Súilleabháin/O'Sullivan – and formed several traditional music groups. Ó Riada died during their second year of college. At UCC she earned bachelor's and master's degrees. The completion of her master's degree coincided with the birth of her first child, Eoin: 'We've one photo at home which is lining the small fellow up beside the thesis – different types of productivity!' Still, she would need to carve out her own career; nothing would be handed to her. Her singing style and art form were unique.

> Look at the music departments [in the early 1990s], they're full of women. It's 90 per cent women and 10 per cent men. Yet where do these women go when you go out? They don't end up composers. As a singer it's different. I was [often] isolated in my work because the nature of my singing is unique – I'm not a classical singer and I'm not a traditional singer. I'm a sort of spiritual singer who might be asked to sing at a funeral like that of Seán MacBride or at a conference on spirituality.

In the 1980s, when she and Mícheál were first living close to Glenstal Abbey, the abbot, Augustine O'Sullivan, who had a great respect for the Irish language and devotion to Mary, facilitated their engagement with the community. As a result, Nóirín's singing relationship with the monks at Glenstal Abbey began in earnest. She traded songs she discovered through her studies for her master's degree. In return, the monks taught her Gregorian chant. Together, they produced several successful albums, including Nóirín's first album *Caoineadh na Maighdine/The Lament of the Virgin* (1980).

In those early professional singing years, during the process of building a reputation as a performer and in addition to her husband's encouragement, it was a woman who provided vital support for Nóirín. Her 'patron' Elinore Detiger, from the Netherlands originally but living in the USA, was part of a wave of women promoting an exploration of feminist spirituality.

> She came up to me at this event arranged by the poet Brendan Kennelly for visiting theologian Matthew Fox … on creation spirituality and said, 'I'm going to take you all over the world. I think it's your time.'

Thereafter, Nóirín began her world tour, first to Iona in Scotland, to Latin America, North America (including a performance at the United Nations), Belgium, the Netherlands, Poland, a performance at the World Summit on the Environment in Rio de Janeiro, Brazil in 1992, and at the Global Women's Conference on women's rights in Beijing, China in 1995, to which Nóirín transported a Brigid's flame lit from the original in Kildare.

> Before all that, I was married to someone in the public domain. It's the downside of being a woman. I was either Mícheál Ó Súilleabháin's wife or people are looking around to see if there are twelve monks behind me. I was still in somebody's shadow. I was sort of weathered by those experiences and had the energy to go out on my own.

Those international engagements, coupled with Elinore's patronage, contributed to Nóirín's growing reputation, helped her to develop her skill and boosted her confidence as an artist. 'Every time I sing one of my deep songs it's kind of healing, kind of visionary. It was giving of my art.' Yet, she wanted more. There was a lack, still.

Thirty years later, on 8 July 2023, I go to Nóirín's house in rural Limerick, divorced from her husband, the late Mícheál, her children grown, with their own children now, so she's a grandmother, too.

> From a personal point of view, I don't recognise myself from that person, thirty years ago. So much has happened on a personal level, it's like looking at a different person, a much wiser person, I hope. I've mellowed in so many ways, taken life as it comes. Living a much more compassionate life, an interfaith life. I've moved on from the Roman Catholic Church.

Nonetheless, Nóirín later explains that in her life now she's also 'maintaining the treasures that I have inherited from the Catholic church'. The name on Nóirín's house, where she's lived for the last seven years, located outside but beside Glenstal Abbey, is 'Imeall', the Irish word for 'edge'.

> I was there with them [the monks], praying and singing with them [for years] ... To this day, one of my best friends is a monk at Glenstal Abbey, Mark Patrick Hederman, who visits me in my home every week.

In 2003, Nóirín completed a ground-breaking doctorate on the theology of listening, for which she coined the word 'theosony': from the Greek 'Theos' (God) and the Latin word 'sonans' (sounding) – the sound of God:

> God is the sound engineer who fine-tunes the organic spiritual melody of each one of us, modifying it to create the most perfect sound of love. My life is a crusade of the sound and the sacred – a mission of pray-sing towards praising.

Later, Nóirín explains that 'living on and off in the monastery of Glenstal Abbey, between 2000 and 2016, was a very rich time for me, for which I am so grateful to the community for allowing me to be there'. However, a time came when she 'found it no longer satisfying. I felt I needed to move on. Something was not right. I needed more', quoting the writer Anaïs Nin by way of explanation: 'The time came when it was more painful to remain in the bud than to blossom.'

Nóirín always wanted to pursue her own ministry – that calling never left her: 'I had the option of doing the humanist route, but I could never say I didn't believe in God. Whereas studying to be an interfaith minister was about all faiths and none.' For two years, she travelled to London to train as an interfaith minister with One Spirit Interfaith Seminary. She later explains that she 'loved every minute of the teaching', before being ordained in 2017.

> On the day that I was ordained, it was one of the most powerful days of my life, I didn't think it would be, on July 27, 2017. A very exciting day and also a very sad day [because ordination could never happen in the Catholic Church].

Nóirín's desire to be a priest, an interfaith minister, a step unavailable to her via the Roman Catholic church, was achieved on her own terms. She continues to remain true to the practices and traditions of her Catholic faith.

The blending of traditions is nothing new in the Irish context and is best understood in terms of the revered place of Brigid, the Celtic goddess and saint, in Irish spiritual practice. The people's devotion to Brigid was so great and so much a part of the fabric of Gaelic society that during the fifth century, when Ireland was Christianised, Brigid was incorporated into the Christian tradition and re-named Saint Brigid.

When Nóirín and her family were at Boston College in 1990, feminist theologian and Dubliner Mary Condren was working on her ThD, a doctorate in theology, at Harvard University.

Author of *The Serpent and the Goddess: Women, religion and power in Celtic Ireland*, Condren's work is probably the most authoritative book on the suppression of the sacred feminine by the emerging Christian Church in Ireland. The serpent in the title refers to the fishtailed woman, a symbol of she who controls fertility, which may explain the myth where St Patrick is purported to have driven the serpents or snakes out of Ireland. Mary Condren argues: 'The form of religion that the Serpent represented was a major threat to the new religion of Israel and to the future of Western civilisation … Goddess religions would have to be overthrown.'[1] So, the goddess Brigit, whose very name means the 'high one' or exalted one, had to be deposed, thereby ensuring that 'women's religious authority was diminished and dismantled'.

Condren highlights the decline of matriarchal power in western civilisation from the 'Age of Eve to the Age of Brigit, then the Age of Mary, to the Age of the Fatherism', to explain the various stages involved in the downgrading of feminine spirituality in Ireland. The downgrading enabled the rise of patriarchal power within the nation state and Christianity, both working hand in hand. When Brigid was incorporated into the Christian tradition she had enormous influence in the early stages of Christianity, with more churches named after her than Mary, the Virgin Mother. However, once the Catholic Church deployed the system of dioceses in the twelfth century, according to Mary Condren, the Virgin Mary became the icon of virginity, the embodiment of controlled female sexuality. Based on her analysis, historically the patriarchal state and Christian church, in their efforts to achieve power, to dominate, downplay the role of women in Irish society and seek to control reproduction.

This focus on power and control is, Condren argues, in direct contrast with pre-Celtic Irish society that operated in terms of matrilineal systems, where the primary concern was on care of the most vulnerable as a measure of success, not violence, strength or control. With the decline in the importance and influence of the goddess Brigid secured, Condren charts a rise in the repression of women. Her book is an invaluable work on women, religion and power in Ireland.

Analysis by the late Seán Ó Duinn, a Benedictine monk at Glenstal Abbey, author of *The Rites of Brigid: Goddess and saint*, which draws on Christian texts, confirms how Brigid was adapted into the Christian tradition.[2] The celebration of Brigid's Day on 1 February, the first day of spring in the Celtic seasonal quarter of Imbolg – literally 'in the belly' – is a direct reference to female fecundity and reproduction. The fact that in the Irish language her day is simply referred to as Lá Fhéile Bríde/Lá 'le Bríde, Brigid's Day, not St Brigid's Day, is evidence of Brigid's pre-Christian existence and her central place in folk culture and customs.

The Irish folk song 'Gabhaim Molta Bríde' (I give praise to Brigid), taught in Irish schools for decades, is a song that Nóirín sings as part of her repertoire. Rituals linked to Brigid connect us to the ideas of transition and transformation, force us to notice nature's cycle, engage us in the magic of wishing for what we desire, starting anew no matter what we have endured through the long winter, while at the same time affording us protection during a time of change. In 1995, when Nóirín travelled to the Fourth World Conference on Women in Beijing, she brought a candle lit from the flame at St Brigid's parish church in Kildare. In 2023, the Irish government designated St Brigid's Day/Imbolc, 1 February, a national holiday, a recognition of the importance of Brigid and her legacy, elevating her to the same stature as St Patrick, the blow-in from Wales, the saint often associated with Ireland.

Gabhaim Molta Bríde/I give praise to Brigid

Gabhaim molta Bride	I am praising Brigid
Ionmhain í le hÉireann	Beloved in Ireland
Ionmhain le gach tír í	Beloved in all countries
Molaimís go léir í	We all praise her

Lóchrann geal na Laighneach	The bright torch of Leinster (province)
'Soilsiú feadh na tíre	Lighting all of Ireland
Ceann ar óghaibh Éireann	Guide to the youth
Ceann na mban ar míne	Guide to women
Tig an gheimhreadh dian dubh	Winter's dark house
Gearradh lena ghéire	Cut us with its sharpness
Ach ar Lá 'le Bríde	But on Brigid's day
Gar dúinn Earrach Éireann	Spring is near
Gabhaim molta Bride	I am praising Brigid
Ionmhain í le hÉireann	Beloved in Ireland
Ionmhain le gach tír í	Beloved in all countries
Molaimís go léir í	We all praise her

As an ordained interfaith minister, Nóirín Ní Riain now conducts rituals on request – marriages, births, deaths and divorces. She also offers spiritual counselling to people seeking the spiritual in their lives. Despite her experience, Nóirín's commitment to Catholic rituals, the Rosary, the Stations of the Cross, the Psalms, remains rock solid. I ask her to explain how this could be when she clearly finds no place for her leadership and ministry within the Catholic Church. She proffers the line that had stayed with me from our conversation thirty years earlier: 'God will look after me.' That rock-solid faith, Nóirín's foundation, gives her strength.

> Yes, it's true. The God of our understanding, whatever that is – a Higher Power, a Higher Source. Sufis would say, 'Listen to the breath of God. Listen beyond the names' – Mahomed, Buddha, Jesus, Krishna. The names get us bogged down. Whereas we all know that we're caught up in this huge cosmic connection. I think it's the lack of that understanding that has us in this state: of lack, of disorder, dis-ease, the lack of a spiritual foundation.

The social context within which Nóirín now conducts her ministry in 2023 has changed radically. To demonstrate the extent of change, I feel it is important to highlight some controversies relating to the physical and sexual abuse of women and children, starting in the 1990s, which cumulatively have contributed to the decimation of the Catholic Church's moral authority in Ireland. While Nóirín does not comment on these controversies, I consider it vital to do so for readers to understand why her spiritual ministry might be attractive in Irish society.

Ireland was once considered the most Catholic country in the world, the island of saints and scholars, the place where monks 'saved civilisation' during the Dark Ages, but according to the 2016 census weekly Mass attendance in Ireland, which stood at 91 per cent in 1975, was down to 36 per cent. In 2023, research conducted by Amárach found that 40 per cent of those who attended weekly Mass before COVID no longer do so. The steady decline in the number of believers and their attendance at major rituals such as weekly Mass in Ireland can be charted from the 1990s, in direct parallel with the revelations of abuse by members of the Catholic Church and institutional cover-ups, dating back many decades.

The late journalist Mary Raftery's dogged determination to uncover the truth in relation to the Catholic Church and the appalling abuse of children resulted in two television documentaries which shocked the nation: *States of Fear* (1999) about children in industrial schools, and *Cardinal Secrets* (2002) about the cover-up in the Catholic Church. Both documentaries were catalysts for the government-commissioned Ryan and Murphy reports published in 2009.

However, this story of abuse dates back even further. From the mid-eighteenth century to 1996, thousands of women and girls in Ireland were sent by their families to work as free labour in convent-run workhouses called Magdalene laundries, financially supported by the state, often because they'd become pregnant outside of marriage. In 2014, work by local historian Catherine

Corless in Tuam, County Galway, brought to light the existence of records relating to 796 infant deaths at a mother and baby home there between 1925 and 1961, with no corresponding burial documents. The Bon Secours Sisters, who ran the home, had placed the infant bodies, the 'Tuam babies', in a series of chambers within an old septic tank on the grounds of the home, where they remained after the nuns departed the building. In 2015, a government-appointed Commission of Investigation into Mother and Baby Homes, including the one at Tuam, was set up, and in 2021 reported that about 9,000 children had died in such homes between 1992 and 1998, double the infant mortality rate in the rest of Ireland for that time. The Irish government then formally apologised for its role in the Magdalene laundries. Despite a redress scheme for survivors, many questions of accountability remain unanswered, with researchers still denied access to certain church records.

Even in 2023, the end point of this book, the controversies surrounding the Catholic Church and its treatment of women and children in its care continue. As Maeve Lewis, then CEO of One in Four (an Irish organisation which advocates for survivors of sexual abuse), put it, Irish people simply found the extent of institutional cover-up 'unforgiveable'.[3]

Nóirín understands that people's trust in the institutional Catholic Church in Ireland has been severely damaged, leaving them searching for meaning elsewhere:

> The church has crumbled, so people don't know where to go. Young people are in an oarless boat. That was all a grand thing long ago [in Ireland] when you were a member of a monastic community, you just put yourself into an oarless boat and let the Divine take you to the shore that you were supposed to be on and start there. Now, people are in an oarless boat and they're in chaos.

I ask her if our experience of COVID and its forced isolation has amplified a spiritual lack in our lives.

> That's the exciting thing about it. There's the opportunity [now]. It will come around in circles and there are great movements happening, antidotes to the so-called 'evil' that is going on. I think Ireland has so much to offer. It will come from here, as it did before, from the 'Land of Saints and Scholars'. It's because we [still] have such connection to the land [the sacredness and healing aspects of the land] … I've developed [it] myself. I've become so much more a part of it.

In her early seventies now, the Reverend Dr Nóirín Ní Riain (her formal title) ministers to an ever-expanding global flock via the internet from her little home 'Imeall' in rural County Limerick.[4] In addition, with her two sons, one located in upstate New York, the other in Limerick, Nóirín organises residential in-person events each year in Ireland called 'Turas d'Anam/Soul

Nóirín Ní Riain, 2023
PHOTO BY THE AUTHOR

Pilgrimage'.[5] These international pilgrims come to learn about Ireland's sacred sites through a programme of activities in counties Limerick, Kerry and Cork.

In 2023, Nóirín branched out with a new transnational venture delivered online over six months called 'Holding the Center'. It's a series of seminars aimed at people in their third phase of life, people who want to live their best spiritual lives while also preparing for life's end. By the power of Zoom, Nóirín leads groups monthly from 'Imeall' in Limerick, while her co-host, John Schuster, a retired psychologist, contributes from his base in the USA. The group is seventy-plus strong, comprised of 'recovering Catholics' and believers of various faiths and none, all hungry for an understanding of ritual, people seeking spiritual guidance in a world of chaos and division. Nóirín Ní Riain draws on her breadth of knowledge of interfaith practices and Celtic spirituality to guide the pilgrims in the oarless boat home.

CHAPTER 4

GARRY HYNES

One of the most popular pieces in the National Gallery of Ireland's portrait collection, according to its director, Dr Caroline Campbell, the first woman to hold the position, is a sculpture of theatre director Garry Hynes, by the artist Vera Klute. In July 2023, the sculpture is part of a new exhibition called *It Took a Century: Women artists and the RHA*, established in recognition of the fact that it took the Royal Hibernian Academy a century to elect the first woman artist, a century to achieve equitable representation in the membership and a century to elect its first woman president. When it comes to women's full participation in some Irish institutions, change can be very slow indeed.

Sculpture at the National Gallery of Ireland, 2017, titled 'Garry Hynes (*b.* 1953), Theatre Director, Co-founder of Druid Theatre'
PHOTO COURTESY OF NGI AND THE ARTIST, VERA KLUTE

Crafted from porcelain and concrete, the sculpture of Garry Hynes sits on a wooden plinth. She's wearing a comfortable cardigan, yet she exudes a professional confidence and drive. When it's not on exhibition, the gallery receives calls and correspondence seeking its return. Irish people admire and like Garry Hynes. They recognise and appreciate her theatrical contributions, over several decades, to our understanding of Ireland, its culture and ourselves. She deserves to be on exhibition in the National Gallery of Ireland. In addition to honorary doctorates from several universities, Garry has received numerous theatrical awards, including a Tony award in 1998 for her direction of *The Beauty Queen of Leenane* in New York, the first woman to achieve such an honour.

The National Gallery's *It Took a Century* exhibition opened in the same month that Garry Hynes and DruidO'Casey launched the world premiere of Seán O'Casey's Dublin trilogy – *The Plough and The Stars*, *The Shadow of a Gunman* and *Juno and the Paycock* – at the Galway International Arts Festival, July 2023.[1] Through this new and ambitious production, marking a century after the Irish nation state 'was reborn in the fires of rebellion and war', Garry and Druid seek to spur national debate. The aim, she explains in an interview with Fintan O'Toole at the Galway Arts Festival, is to draw parallels between an Irish past and its present.

> I don't know of any country which has its origin story as a nation state so clearly chronicled by a great writer for the theatre. In a fairly unique way, they actually tell the story of the founding of the Irish state, so that we do them in chronological order: When *The Plough and the Stars* opens, it's autumn 1915, by the second act it's 1916, the Easter Rising. Then the two plays that follow (*Shadow of a Gunman*, *Juno and the Paycock*), cover the War of Independence and the Civil War.[2]

Tickets are snapped up by avid audiences in Galway, Belfast and Dublin for performances in June, July and August, before the production travels to two cities in the USA, New York and Ann

Arbor. I manage to secure a ticket to a back-to-back performance of the three plays at the Skirball Center in New York on 7 October 2023.

It's been a long haul from Ballaghaderreen, County Roscommon, where Garry was born and lived for her first five years. The family moved to Monaghan and later Galway for her father's job as CEO of a vocational education committee. An eldest child, it is not surprising that her work revolves around leadership, the essence of her role as a director. From her early years she immersed herself in English-language books and rebelled against her parents' decision to speak Irish at home.

> My life has been defined by books, by reading. I remember I desperately wanted to read before I could. I remember looking at the newspaper, knowing that my father and mother could make sense of it and I couldn't, thinking how incredible it could be. I remember looking at the death columns and thinking that someday I would understand what it meant.

That early desire to decipher the true meaning of a text provides some insight into why she was drawn to the role of artistic director in the world of theatre – to understand a play, have a vision of how it should be realised, to gather others and collaborate around a shared vision and present the whole to an audience, so that they too have an avenue into the creation of the playwright.

When I first interviewed Garry Hynes in 1992, she was working as the first woman artistic director of Ireland's national theatre, the Abbey, a position she held from 1991 to 1994, with some challenges along the way. The Abbey is laden with associations to the emergence of the Irish nation state, the place where a riot broke out during a performance of O'Casey's *The Plough and the Stars* in 1926. We talked about New York, its energy, its offerings. I had recently returned to Ireland after attending graduate school in America to become a research associate at Trinity College Dublin, an Irish institution with its own set of associations –

Protestant, British – a place where Catholics were banned from studying until 1970.

When Garry was a student at University College Galway (UCG, now the University of Galway) she spent three summers in New York working on a J1 student visa: 'I went to New York the first time when I was 17. I fell in love with the place. I'd go at the start of June until October every year.' She went to every possible theatrical performance, soaked up the *avant garde*, witnessed risk-taking in many art forms, and appreciated quality when she encountered it. Each October on her return to Galway she would apply what she'd learned across the Atlantic to her work with the Drama Society at UCG. After four years at university, in the summer of 1975, Garry and her colleagues Marie Mullen and Mick Lally established Druid Theatre, the first professional theatre in Galway city. They came upon the name from the *Asterix* strip in *The Irish Times*.

> I basically didn't want to stop being involved in the theatre. Where was I to go and what was I to do? I'd no sense of a profession of the theatre, hardly any at all, and the notion of actually trying to get into professional theatre was about as remote as you can imagine. I was working with a number of people with whom I wanted to continue working. We all wanted to continue doing it.

Amateur actors from the UCG Drama Society and others from the Irish-language (Gaelic) theatre An Taibhdhearc ('ghostly vision') joined Marie, Mick and Garry for the founding season of Druid Theatre, performed at the Jesuit Hall in Galway city. Garry directed three plays: *The Loves of Cass Maguire* (Brian Friel), *The Playboy of the Western World* (J.M. Synge) and *It's a Two-Foot-Six-Inches-Above-the-Ground World* (Kevin Laffan).

At the end of the summer's run, Mick Lally arranged a leave of absence from his teaching job so that Druid could plan a year of productions. They were risking a great deal, including a bank loan for 500 pounds. All three collaborators, Garry, Marie and Mick, would now have to survive financially from their artistic efforts. Druid simply had to work.

> We made one, what I think looking back on it now, was an absolutely crucial decision. We decided we would pay ourselves a wage at the end of the week, regardless. We paid ourselves two pounds a week pocket money. Clearly, a certain element of the social services of this country were being used to subsidise the arts, quite properly.

With success after success, Druid received grants from the Arts Council, initially 3,000 pounds and by the 1990s, fifteen years into the company's existence, the grants increased to 200,000 pounds annually, an indicator of the troupe's growing reputation and recognition for quality theatrical productions. 'The company became very established and highly successful in the early 1980s to mid-1980s. As soon as that happened, it started being over.'

Fifteen years of productions with Druid seemed to be enough, including performances of two of her own plays, *The Pursuit of Pleasure*, based on the life of Oscar Wilde, and *Island Protected by a Bridge of Glass*, about the legendary pirate queen Granuaile in sixteenth-century Ireland. The latter included an original score by De Dannan, led by fiddler Frankie Gavin, who performed with the company, a combination that won first prize at the Edinburgh Festival's Fringe First in 1980. Nonetheless, a sense of disenchantment had set in, and Garry sought out new experiences beyond Druid. First, she worked at the Abbey in a short-term, freelance position, and later The Royal Shakespeare Company, before she was offered the plum job as the first woman appointed artistic director at the Abbey, a contract position that ran from 1990 to '93. Her elevation to the position at the Abbey was hard-won during a time when few women had an opportunity to work at leadership level in any sphere, including theatre.

Garry's job leading an institution so centrally associated with the foundation of the Irish state meant that her work was highly scrutinised. The newspapers reported on her every decision. She was now an employee of the state, a public servant. It was not all plain sailing. Reports in the Irish newspapers were many and mainly negative, despite the hugely successful run of Brian Friel's *Dancing at Lughnasa*, for example, during her tenure.

The headline on a piece published in *The Irish Times* on 7 April 1993 explains much about Garry's departure: 'Hynes to Break with Abbey because of Rift with Board'.[3] It describes the tensions within an institution with a 'chronically underused permanent acting company, which the theatre seems able neither to employ nor to dissolve with decency'. Ultimately, Hynes argued that the board had 'never accepted either the principle of the need for reform or the urgency of it'. The article points out that at its core, the controversy involved forces that were 'hostile to particular [unspecified] changes', even though she'd accepted the position based on her belief that the institution was 'in need of substantial reform'. In 1993, her final programme at the Abbey included 'six new plays in as many months … an exciting and important one [programme] for the theatre'. According to Woodworth's 1993 *Irish Times* article, her artistic directorship 'ran into controversy with a radical interpretation of Seán O'Casey's *The Plough and the Stars* in 1991'. This experience is an interesting historical marker, given Garry's desire to stage the DruidO'Casey trilogy in 2023.

The theatre was then, as now, a tough place for women. In 1990s Ireland, a woman with a clear mind about what she wanted could be a force in any area of employment, especially someone shaping the direction of Ireland's national theatre. After her time at the Abbey, Garry considered heading to America, but instead she accepted an invitation to return to Druid where she once again thrived in her role of artistic director. At our first meeting, she described the role of women in theatre, based on her experience in the 1990s at the Abbey:

> There are less good acting roles for women than for men. Their [women's] status as creators is good. Their status when it comes to any set of responsibilities, management, or decisions like that, is not good. So, my feeling is that their [women's] position in the world of theatre, and it's a feeling I have on the position of women generally, while on the face of it [the context] is seemingly quite liberal and open, it's just as bad as it is everywhere else.

Given her analysis of the state of women in theatre in the early 1990s, was she proactive in ensuring women's greater participation, especially playwrights?

> We [the Abbey] had a series of women's plays last year [1991], and I'm considering a women's season over the next six months or so, yes. I'm not sure I'm fully able to defend it if somebody puts up a coherent attack on the notion. We have to do something.

It seems Garry Hynes made some attempt to address the issue of women's participation in activities at Ireland's national theatre in the 1990s, when she was in charge. However, this issue of women's participation would fester and explode in 2016 when Abbey director Fiach Mac Conghail unveiled his programme, *Waking the Nation*, to mark 100 years since the Irish Revolution in 1916. Out of ten plays scheduled, only one was written by a woman. Mac Conghail's decision seemed even more ludicrous at a time of renewed public debate and re-evaluation of the role of women in the 1916 Rising. His response to the criticisms, posted on Twitter (when the social media platform functioned as a lively forum for public debate), was: 'Them's the breaks.' By November, women's anger at the gender inequality at Ireland's national theatre became harnessed into a social movement – *Waking the Feminists* – which organised events across the country, forced the Abbey to devise guiding principles on gender equality and caused ripple effects across the arts in Ireland.

In August 2023, thirty years after our first meeting, Garry Hynes and I sit down again in Dublin shortly before DruidO'Casey heads to New York for its final run there and in Ann Arbor in October. Now in her seventieth year, this production might well be considered her swansong as Druid's artistic director. Her choice of work is apt. In 2023, just about 100 years on from the plays' conception and the establishment of the Irish nation state, this theatrical journey continues to be relevant, a chilling critique of modern Ireland. Garry Hynes knows that drama can be a catalyst for national conversations. The plays, set in Dublin's tenements, point to the lost opportunities of Ireland's revolution because modern Dublin is in the throes of a massive housing crisis, unprecedented homelessness, a message not lost on audiences. In 2023, families are living in tents by the Grand Canal, refugees are crowded in requisitioned hotels, even though the government has over 10 billion euros surplus in its coffers. Therefore, a growing inequality in Irish society in modern times – with housing and health crises – makes the staging of O'Casey's plays so timely. This is the context for Garry Hynes' direction of O'Casey's genius, the Dublin trilogy, the perfect catalyst to spur people to interrogate Ireland's current *state of chassis*.

> It's terrifying … The fact that O'Casey brought to the stage the lives of poor people, deprived people, the people who lived in the tenements, and they were seen to have emotions and needs and a life, the same as a king or queen would in another play … I wanted to find a way to work with the plays that showed the art of it, not just the fact that he himself knew poverty.

A committed socialist, O'Casey's plays were the first to seriously foreground Dublin's working-class communities in three key moments in Irish history: 1923 (*Shadow* – set during the War of Independence), 1924 (*Juno* – set during the Civil War) and 1926 (*The Plough* – set during the Easter Rising 1916). The plays critiqued the arguments of nationalists because from O'Casey's point of view, nationalists lacked a commitment to socialism, to addressing the poverty and social class inequalities in Ireland. On the fourth night of the original performance of *The Plough and the Stars*, in 1926, a riot broke out in the Abbey Theatre, and later that year O'Casey headed for England where he made his lifelong home. Encountered through the lens of 2023, the plays question the social cost of Ireland's economic success. Writing in *The Irish Times*, Fintan O'Toole (5 August 2023) remarked in his review of DruidO'Casey that 'the test of whether a nation is really proud of itself is whether or not it can bear to confront its own most shameful realities'.

Several strong women inhabit O'Casey's works, linked, according to Garry Hynes, to his experience of his mother, to whom he dedicates one of the plays – 'to the gay laugh of my mother at the gate of the grave'. Garry's own mother was an important anchor in her life, even if they sparked off one another, as mothers and daughters do. She died in 2021. 'We were close. We'd fight like hell as well, but we were close.'

I ask her to reflect on the direct relevance of O'Casey's works to an Ireland in 2023:

> O'Casey was fiercely political! Unfortunately, the sort of politics he represented was out of favour – with money and the McQuaids of the time [John Charles McQuaid was the then conservative archbishop of Dublin]. As they say [about the Easter Rising in 1916], 'the wrong men died'. Ireland is a better place now, yes. There's more opportunity, but people are still incredibly poor. One of the consequences of the dominance of the church [in the past] is that there isn't an inherent moral code, a civic moral code. Our morality was imposed on us by a church from the outside. And then when that's gone, or it doesn't mean anything to people, where does it leave you in terms of good and bad, right and wrong?

Despite this lack, Garry Hynes' analysis includes examples of positive social change in Ireland in the thirty years since our first meeting, including the introduction of legislation. She and her partner availed of civil partnership prior to the marriage equality referendum, worried that it might not pass. 'One of the things that has happened to facilitate change is wealth. Ireland was a very poor country. It has become a fairly wealthy country. It can afford to be more tolerant.'

Another theme relevant to a changed Ireland is the level of racial and ethnic diversity, reflected in the DruidO'Casey troupe, too, with two Black actors in its cast of eighteen.

> Diversity [in Ireland] is huge and it's great! Clearly, we have begun to reflect that diversity in our theatre. At the same time, we have to remember that the kind of diversity there is in the US came from slavery, and in the UK from colonialism – very different to our diversity. We skipped from the colonisation by the British empire to advance the Catholic empire – much more dangerous, because they came into our heads, whereas the other was financial and economic.

While acknowledging the litany of damages done by the Catholic Church in Irish society, especially in relation to women's lives – the plethora of sexual abuse cases, the Magdalene laundries, etc. – based on her experience, Garry Hynes wishes to highlight the positive contributions made by individual religious to Irish society.

> It won't happen now, but it will happen sometime soon where you're going to have histories and stories about the religious in Ireland since the nineteenth century in a way that won't all be about the awful things, but some of the very good things done, and good people. Some of the nuns who taught me were people I admired and ever since I became an adult, I continue to admire.

Garry's analysis is a reminder to distinguish between the role of the institutional Catholic Church in these awful controversies and her experience of the positive contribution of individuals within the church who were/are deeply committed to a sense of social justice, a life of service. By way of example, she describes a pivotal encounter with a nun who facilitated her first experience of directing a play. Garry, aged eleven, was in fifth class in primary school in Monaghan, at the St Louis convent. Her teacher, Sr Mary Josephine, encouraged her to direct the play and arranged for the young Garry to 'tour' the other classes in the school. This timely intervention remained with her all her life. Their relationship was so important to Garry that she maintained a correspondence with Sr Mary Josephine up to the time of the nun's death. The memory of her eleven-year-old self directing for the first time offers the perfect segue for me to ask Garry to describe the process of directing a play.

> Quite simply, there's this very, very strange process called rehearsing a play. It's the same process whether you're doing it in a school classroom at eleven years of age or you're doing it like the O'Casey trilogy. In effect, you're the leader of that process – in visionary and executive leadership. You have to ensure that the grounds are there for the piece to be done, to be presented to an audience and engage with that audience. The thing about it is that you can't direct on your own. I have to collaborate. It's the only way to work. Yes, I am the group leader; I lead the process. The more that I can communicate, and the actors can communicate with each other and with me and with the crew – the more they do that, the better the play, the performance of it – connecting it all. There are seven actors in a company of eighteen [DruidO'Casey] that I have never worked with before and that's been absolutely wonderful.

As with any team, trust is at the heart of the theatrical process, mutual trust, born out of respect for each person's contribution, on and off the stage – and always one captain whose position of authority ultimately holds sway.

During the pandemic years, Garry knew that Druid had to be innovative, to use technology to facilitate the company to be immersed in its practice, to perform for its loyal audience members, to enable art to transcend above the tragedy of COVID. Under Garry's direction, the company performed outdoors in Coole Park, Galway, all around the estate, a series of Lady Gregory's one-act plays. In addition, Druid used its presence across various social media platforms to strategically market its offerings, to communicate with its audience.

Now in her seventieth year, and with no successor identified to lead Druid Theatre, it seems as though this DruidO'Casey production may well be Garry's last major work to be taken on tour to the USA. At the Skirball Center by Washington Square Park in New York, the performance I witness of the DruidO'Casey trilogy seems to be well received by the mostly older Irish-American audience. At the performance of each of the three plays I notice many empty seats in the auditorium, filled

Garry Hynes, 2023
PHOTO BY THE AUTHOR

at various times by New York University drama students. Perhaps audiences abroad, especially members of the Irish diaspora, are not as attuned as audiences in Ireland to Garry Hynes' motive for staging the trilogy now as a way of critiquing the sores of society in modern Ireland.

In an interview with *The New York Times* (4 October 2023), Garry explains that in O'Casey's plays 'the domestic is reflecting on what's outside. So, you're hearing about all the things going on out in the streets. They're marching. They're striking. They're killing people … and inside they're fighting.'[4] Given the timeframe of this book, 1993–2023, her words seem prescient as the world witnesses unprecedented riots and destruction on O'Connell Street in the heart of Ireland's capital in November 2023. Life overtakes drama – this time.

CHAPTER 5

OLWEN GILL

The multi-million-euro ferry I board on a glorious day in June 2023 at the Galway quayside takes us some thirty miles west to Inis Mór, an island about eight miles long and two miles wide, the largest of the three Aran islands. It operates during the tourist season from May to October. All around me on this modern vessel I hear a cacophony of languages and accents. Among the passengers are not just curious overseas tourists wishing to explore one of Ireland's tourism gems, but also various groups from Ireland's migrant population. A few Southeast Asian families are clustered together talking in English about the train journey from their home in Dublin to Galway city. Beside them, a mother and two daughters wearing hijabs sit together speaking in Arabic. Of course there are American tourists on board, too, evident from their accents, with two Black families among them. Europe is represented by the Italians – over a dozen men in one group, all wearing recently purchased tweed caps, rustic clothing that somehow seems very cool and fashionable atop their handsome faces. This one ferry journey seems to encapsulate the extent and nature of change in Ireland – the ethnic and racial diversity, the magnificent transport vessel – and above the din of passenger chat, the crew are speaking to one another *as Gaeilge*/in Irish. We are, after all, in a Gaeltacht, an Irish-speaking area of Ireland, in a nation where Irish is the first official language of the state.

It's high season for tourists and tourism has always been a major contributor to Inis Mór's economy. However, unlike in the past, when people stayed for days or weeks, my companions on the ferry are day-trippers, the main category of tourist now. They rent bicycles, hire a driver with pony and trap or hop on a bus to bring them around the island, including the obligatory visit to its famous Dún Aengus archaeological site, some 3,500 years old. These days, most tourists spend only a few hours on Inis Mór because that's what twenty-first-century tourists seem to demand before heading on to the next 'must see' place. It's not about immersion in a culture or a place or even Irish Americans finding their roots. It's not a Synge-style encounter with Aran culture. It's pressure-driven tourism. After a speedy spin by whatever means around the island, a guided tour of Dún Aengus, there's just about time to grab a bite to eat at one of the few restaurants or at the aptly-named X trailer café, or to browse the touristy shops around Kilronan that sell Aran sweaters, all these activities completed before boarding the late afternoon ferry back to Galway via another notable tourism site, the Cliffs of Moher, an obligatory return route.

As we dock at Kilronan harbour, I see that Olwen Gill awaits me. Despite the decades since we last met, I still recognise her. She smiles and waves as I descend from the ferry, then drives me to her home situated in Killeany, up above the main village of Kilronan, a stunning location offering a magnificent view of the harbour from her living room.

View from Olwen's home towards Kilronan, Inis Mór, 2023
PHOTO BY THE AUTHOR

To conduct my first set of interviews with women on the island in 1992, I'd travelled not by boat, but on a small ten-seater plane from Carnmore, outside Galway city. In my bag I'd carried a cassette tape recorder, batteries, notebooks and a copy of Tim Robinson's magnificent study mapping the island's placenames/*logainmneacha*, folklore, wildlife, flora and fauna – *Stones of Aran: Pilgrimage* (1986). On that memorable twenty-minute flight I recall that the airport's runway on Inis Mór consisted of a grassy patch of land, the outline of the landing area indicated by a border of whitewashed stones. My travelling companions then were islanders – *ag caint as Gaeilge*/speaking in Irish – returning from Galway city. The cost of the flight for them was subsidised by the state as its commitment to 'lifeline' transport services for Ireland's inhabited offshore islands. I sat to the rear of the plane, the seats beside me laden with plastic-wrapped blocks containing cartons of milk and loaves of shop white bread. I was amazed that the locals needed to source these staples on the mainland. During that visit in 1992, I interviewed five women on Inis Mór, based on the recommendation of the local schoolteacher, whom I knew. Back then, I was uncertain how the project would ultimately take shape and never imagined it would be so long before I returned. Unfortunately, by 2023, many of those women, born and bred on the island, were long dead. However, the interviews, conducted in Irish and English, capturing their words and points of view on island life, were at least preserved on cassette tapes which I'd arranged to archive so that others might access them in the future.

Olwen Gill is a 'blow-in' who married an island man, Michael Gill, her childhood sweetheart. Dublin-born Olwen Coogan attended an Irish-speaking primary school and spent three months of every summer on Inis Mór. The family rented out their Dublin house to enable them to rent another on the island. Her father, journalist and writer Tim Pat Coogan, would join them for the month of August. As we did in our first interview, we spoke in Irish and in English. I offer quotes in both languages here. Having spent a lifetime living on the island, I assumed that

Olwen's original outsider status afforded her a keen eye to notice the changes that had taken place in island life in the intervening decades.

Always drawn to the sea, Olwen planned to study marine biology at the university in Galway. After finishing secondary school, she took a year out to work in Denmark and during that time away, her father applied, on her behalf, for a place on a teacher-training course at Carysfort Training College, then run by the Sisters of Mercy religious order. For young women in 1970s Ireland, training as a national teacher was a big deal – offering a high-status position in the community and the guarantee of a teaching job on graduation. You had to be smart to get a place, too. She did, but it wasn't what Olwen wanted. She began her second year at Carysfort and then left. She headed for Inis Mór to be with Michael, who was teaching at the local second-level vocational school. That was 1979. She was nineteen and willing to work at anything. What followed was a succession of jobs, mostly in bed-and-breakfasts where she helped to cook and clean during the six-month tourist season. She and Michael lived together for a year before they got married in 1980. In 1989, they bought a house, and set up their own B&B business, with the additional offering of an evening meal provided as an incentive to attract guests. It was tough work, especially once their first child Thomond was born in 1983, followed later by Nóinín in 1987 and their last child, Peadar, in 1994.

> Caithfidh tú eirí ar leath uair tar éis a seacht, b'fhéidir níos luath, chun an boird a leagadh. Deinim leite agus scones ar maidin, agus fíor juice – gach aon rud úr – tógann siad é sin faoi deara. Chuile bhliain thagaidís ar ais. Ansin, caithfidh tú glanadh suas – na seomraí a glanadh. Ag a dó a clog, téim go dtí an trá. Tosnaím an dinnéar ag a cúig.
>
> [You have to be up early, half seven, or earlier. I prepare porridge and scones and real orange juice – all from scratch – they notice that. Many of our guests returned year after year.

After that, you have to clean up and clean the rooms. At two o'clock I go to the beach. Then I start the dinner at five.]

When we first met in 1992, Olwen was thirty-two, 'le mortgage mór/with a big mortgage', and two small children. She had to put her all into the B&B to make it work because there were seven or eight houses near her also offering B&B. Ever the entrepreneur, and in the lingo of business, she'd diversified into 'saoire sláintiúil/health holidays' with the help of her mother, Cherry, a trained beautician, offering various treatments. Olwen showcased local foods – from her garden and from the sea – and brought the guests on long walks around the island, explaining the unique flora and fauna, archaeological treasures and local sights. The national television station, RTÉ, profiled the operation, which resulted in even more business. However, only one of her six guest bedrooms was en suite, equipped with its own private bathroom. The others had handbasins only, so that guests had to share two bathrooms. Everyone wanted the room with the en suite. It was crunch time for the family. They could borrow 'big money' and invest in the business to upgrade the bedrooms by installing showers and toilets, but they were competing with neighbours who had purpose-built houses, where every guest room was en suite. Even in the early 1990s, visitors' expectations had changed. Letting go of the B&B was not a hardship for Olwen once the ferryboat company set up two hostels offering an all-in package of transport to and around the island and accommodation. There was no way that she could compete.

A series of jobs followed, demonstrating her capacity to put her hand to anything, especially work with flexible hours, while she was rearing her young family. She set up a 'naíonra', an Irish-language pre-school, in 1983, before the birth of her first child, Thomond. She worked with the island's co-op on its recycling scheme WASTE and later as a fitness instructor at the co-op's gym before becoming a substitute teacher in the local primary and secondary schools. Now, in 2023, she's a tour guide at

Dún Aengus during the tourist season, her ninth year in a job that she loves.

Born in 1960, when Olwen first came to the island as a child she remembers the simplicity of life in a place with no electricity, where they went daily to the well for water. She tells me that Inis Mór was connected to the national grid in 1975, during Ireland's rural electrification programme that started in the late 1940s. The only telephone on the island in the 1960s was located at the post office, which offered a wind-up, operator-assisted service. As a result, there were no electricity poles or telephone wires to cut across the pristine views of this beautiful, barren landscape with no trees, but lots of stone walls, each one still named after the original builder. She remembers the bus coming to the island, too, an innovation that required the roads to be tarred for the first time.

> The electricity came after we got a plane, [which was] in 1972 or so. Now [2023], the changes are phenomenal. When we were kids [1960s] there would be loads of ponies and traps on the pier to bring tourists to Dún Aengus, the men in their pampooties [handmade shoes] and their braideens [woven belts] and their caps. Then the buses, and they got bigger – nine-seater, sixteen-seater, now they're thirty-seaters. There are thousands of bikes, all owned by the same guy. They all go in the same direction, during the same hours. The B&Bs are gone.

The most pressing issue on the island, according to Olwen, is housing, or the lack of it, due in large part to strict planning regulations. With its designated status as a unique ecological island, Inis Mór's development is in a bind: how do you ensure that young families rearing their children *as Gaeilge*/in Irish can build a home and still preserve the natural beauty and treasures of a unique ecosystem? It's a question that has directly impacted many of the island's families. Issues around planning, long-term rental and accessing a mortgage are also, Olwen tells me, extremely problematic.

> The council [Galway County Council] moved families to the mainland for housing. There's a big need for it [housing]. People are leaving. I could name several families that in the last ten years have left the island with young children because they can't get planning permission [to build] and they can't rent a house long-term [due to the focus on tourism and short-term lets]. There are derelict houses on the island, but you can't get a mortgage to do up a derelict house. This is a microcosm of what's happening everywhere else [in Ireland].

With the global economic crash in 2008, Ireland's open economy was particularly hard hit not least because of the banks' poor lending practices, but also because of an over-reliance on construction as a fueller of economic growth. Entire housing estates, even partially finished ghost estates, were bought up by global vulture funds who also laid claim to cheap apartment blocks in urban areas. The decision then by the Irish government to back the banks with an open-ended guarantee meant that that the nation was forced to borrow financial aid from the Troika – the European Commission, the International Monetary Fund and the European Central Bank – who insisted on austerity measures. The result was a set of massive cutbacks in state funding in a range of areas, including housing. Since then, Ireland has never properly addressed the shortfall in housing, which was made all the more acute in the 2020s by the demands of a burgeoning population. In addition, a concentration by those in political power on delivery of short-term rather than longer-term goals is a contributing factor. The pragmatism of national politics, driven by the necessity to form coalition governments, requires compromise among all political parties and independents. This has been the reality for decades. With over a million and a half people living in Dublin, the media and politicians seem focused on the acute housing and homeless crisis in the nation's capital. Therefore, the acute housing shortage on Inis Mór in 2023 merely reflects the national housing crisis and lack of housing stock. It's an issue that has impacted the island's population which at its peak, in 1841, was 2,500, but by 2023 had dropped to 800 people.

> When I was a kid, everyone would have six kids – six would be a small family. People married much younger and stayed here. Then the kids would get jobs on the mainland. As the years went on, they started doing the Leaving Cert here and the kids went to university and didn't come back. In the 1980s, people went to America mainly. Now, lots of kids from here are in Australia, an awful lot.

Significant emigration has been a feature of island life since at least the nineteenth century. However, as parents realised that not having English was a handicap to their children's prospects abroad, many families began to speak English, to prepare them for the boat.

> Nuair a d'fhág daoine an oileán gan Béarla, bhí sé deachair orthu. Chuadar go Meiriceá, go Sasana, agus ní rabhadar in ann fógraí a léamh. Dúirt siad nach d'tarlódh sé sin arís.
>
> [When people left the island without English, it was very difficult on them. They went to America, to England, and they were not able to read the signs. They [parents] said that that would not happen again.]

Clearly, Inis Mór needs young families to stay, to rear children through the medium of Irish, to re-populate its schools and ensure survival of its rich language heritage, but it's a delicate balance to respond to the housing crisis and the island's tourism needs and to preserve its unique ecological heritage. Tourism is its life-blood, yet the island's community relies on a septic system for its waste treatment in a place where water sources must be carefully monitored for quality. You cannot disgorge hundreds of people from ferryboats for a few hours daily for six months and expect the island's sanitation infrastructure to withstand it: 'There are not enough public toilets. There definitely aren't for the amount of people visiting.' It is not just a matter of the sustainability of the island's tourism industry; more importantly, planning and housing is determining its very future as a viable place to live.

> I'd say planning has a lot to do with it. It's really difficult even for kids living here now to build on their own land, and they can't always get it [planning permission], because the island is an area of scientific conservation – the nature of the rock is porous, the plants are protected, the rock itself is protected.

Building materials must be ferried to the island. Nothing can be sourced locally for construction.

All three of Olwen's children, fluent Irish speakers, left the island to attend university in Dublin and all have made lives for themselves on the mainland. Her daughters are both teachers in Dublin. Her son works in Belfast where he's been involved with the film *Kneecap*, about Irish-language rappers, which got rave reviews at the Sundance Film Festival. Olwen's second daughter, Nóinín, a teacher at Gaelscoil an Chuilinn in Tyrellstown, Dublin 15, 'the most diverse population in Dublin', was staying with Olwen and Michael for the year in 2023. Nóinín's husband, a data analyst, was able to work remotely. Rearing their children through Irish, they wanted them to have the experience of total language immersion in a Gaeltacht area, in Nóinín's home place, and precious time with grandparents Olwen and Michael in a beautiful location.

> They bought a house in Blanchardstown, off the plans, in an estate, five years ago. Now it's apartment blocks surrounding it. They're overlooked whichever way you look. She's taking time off, extending maternity leave, a career break. He can work from home.

Therefore, Olwen's three children bring their fluency in Irish and their love of the language to endeavours in different urban areas in Ireland where use of Irish has experienced a revival, especially in places with a Gaelscoil. A contributing factor to the revival success has been the establishment of TG4, the state's Irish-language television station, in 1996. TG4 and its radio equivalent, Raidió na Gaeltachta, facilitate communication between Gaeltacht communities, but have also proven to be enormous assets to those seeking to learn and promote use of the Irish language, irrespective of location in Ireland or abroad. Olwen sees TG4 as a perfect complement to and a key resource for the Gaelscoil movement, where parents – not the state, not the church – establish, organise and control Irish-language primary and secondary schools, most located in urban areas.

> Anois tá TG4 agus na Gaelscoileanna [againn] – is rud mór mílteach é sin ar fud na tíre. Tá an iarrachas ag teacht ó na tuismitheoirí. Ní leis an eaglais an foirgneamh. Na daoine óga, níl an Gaeilge brútha orthu mar a bhíodh. Tá céim ar aghaidh tugadh don Gaeilge – ní teanga daoine bochta san áit iargúlta é.
>
> [Now there's TG4 and the Gaelscoileanna – it's a massive movement throughout the country. The demand is coming from the parents. The church doesn't own the building. And the young people don't feel tormented about it, like they used to. Now it's progressive. It's no longer the language of poor people in remote places.]

However, while it appears that the number of people speaking Irish has grown nationally, they are speaking it less frequently. In the CSO's 2022 census, approximately 40 per cent of the population reported that they could speak Irish, about 1.9 million people, with only 10 per cent reporting that they could speak 'very well', 32 per cent could speak it 'well', while 55 per cent could not speak it well.[1] These findings illustrate that even though Irish is the first official language of the state and even though the language is taught in schools, more than half the population, 60 per cent, does not speak Irish. In 2022, there were 106,000 people living in Gaeltacht areas, i.e. designated parts of Ireland where Irish is the first language in the community, mostly located on the west coast, places such as Inis Mór, that receive a range of supports from the state to preserve the language. An interesting trend, according to CSO data, is that while there are now more people living in the Gaeltacht areas – up 7 per cent in April 2022 compared to April 2016 – they are not Irish-language speakers. The proportion of Irish speakers in Gaeltacht areas continues to decrease, from 69 per cent in 2011 to 66 per cent in 2022. These findings suggest that recent residents in the Gaeltachtaí are not Gaelgeoirí (speakers of Irish), which is an issue in terms of community cohesion and a challenge to the state's efforts to promote language usage.

For generations, families on Inis Mór lived off the fruits of the ocean, fishing from wooden-framed, tarred, canvas-covered rowing boats called currachs. According to myth, fishermen deliberately didn't learn to swim, accepting their fate and loath to struggle with the ocean if they got into difficulty. Better to have a swift drowning. It was the reason given for the different design patterns that evolved on Aran sweaters – a means of identifying members of particular fishing families if their bodies washed ashore. It's a story told in the video running non-stop in the sweater shop at Kilronan. Olwen disagrees with this theory completely. She thinks it had more to do with fishermen's modesty in Catholic Ireland, their reluctance to strip off in order to learn how to swim. It's an interesting perspective, new to me.

In an acknowledgement of the centrality of fishing to the island community, the Irish government supported the move away from currachs to big sail boats like nobbies and zulus in the 1950s, then later, trawlers, like the ards and schees. However, once Ireland joined the European Economic Community (later to become the European Union) in 1973, the fishing grounds around Ireland became subject to EU regulation and access was divided among member states. As a result, in the 2020s it's difficult for Inis Mór's fishing families to compete with mega-trawlers, often Spanish in origin and with Filipino crews – 'factory ships that hoover the catch, fillet and freeze it on board' and then proceed directly to market. Olwen's neighbours, families who have fished all their lives, have decided they can no longer make a living from the ocean. 'Once the boats go, the knowledge goes with them.' She is deeply disturbed by this pattern and its consequences for her community.

> Three island boats were decommissioned in the last few weeks [June 2023]. It's very sad. Overfishing is a big part of it, but government policy is the worst part of it. The small trawler can't compete, can't go out as far [as Spanish mega-trawlers]. My neighbour who decommissioned a couple of weeks ago, he's fished all his life. His last boat he's had for twenty-three years.

Island communities have campaigned under the banner of Comharchumann Forbartha Árann/Aran Development Co-Op to pressure Údarás na Gaeltachta/Gaeltacht Authority and public representatives to respond to their basic need to make a living, as generations have done, in their home place. Fianna Fáil politician Éamon Ó Cuív, TD, was a major supporter of the 43-million-euro pier development at Kilronan on Inis Mór, opened twelve years ago. It's an innovation that Olwen supports, because it ensures safety for the ferries and fishing boats. An enormous project logistically, not least because all the building materials had to be sourced and transported from the mainland. A recent EU Horizon 2020 project, REACT – Renewable Energy for Self-Sustainable Island Communities – funded the installation of 250 solar panels on public and private buildings. These are all positive developments. However, just a few years ago, a plan to grant permission for a salmon farm at Inis Mór to a company with a poor environmental track record was a step too far for the community, who organised a successful campaign to reverse the decision.[2] Therefore, Olwen and her community have learned that there is always a need for vigilance.

> The government in its wisdom gave a licence for a salmon fish farm, the biggest in the world, to be positioned not a mile off our shore, operated by an international company whose wrecking of places with impunity all over the world [is well documented]. There were huge campaigns, a national campaign, it wasn't just the island.

With fishing no longer a viable proposition to support local families, tourism is now the main industry on the island. However, as Olwen explains, the B&Bs are gone and it's difficult to survive on an industry that operates for six months of the year with day-trippers as the main source of revenue. Those involved in tourism have adapted: 'There's luxury glamping facilities now and the hotel has pods', accommodations that are perceived as temporary structures by the authorities and therefore not subject to strict planning regulations. The most recent development in island tourism has been the arrival of yachts that anchor at the island for a few days, using the location as a staging area for yacht races in 2017 and again in 2023 – the West of Ireland Offshore Racing Association (WIORA) championships. In addition, pleasure craft from France, Spain and Italy anchor off the island and come ashore for entertainment, adding a cosmopolitan flavour to the conversations in the local pubs.

Nowadays, it's highly likely that the person working behind the bar or shop counter on Inis Mór is a migrant resident in Ireland. With the expansion of the EU in 2004, Polish migrants were drawn to different parts of Ireland, including its islands. On Inis Mór they work in tourism and other jobs on the island: 'They are still here, married here with children who go to school through Irish. In summer they work in the hotel. There wouldn't be work in the winters.' With limited accommodation on the island, migrant workers in the island's shops and cafés must secure room and board as well as a job on Inis Mór. However, as Olwen repeats often in her description of changes she's witnessed, the island is a 'microcosm' of life on the mainland, and the lack of housing is the number one issue on Inis Mór, as it is in many parts of Ireland.

In her lifetime, Olwen has witnessed many changes, including changes in social legislation that directly impacted her own family of origin. Her parents separated when she was an adult, though they are now 'the best of buddies'. Still, she understood first-hand the need for change.

> You wouldn't talk about it – separation – in the past. With divorce, you'd read about stars [divorcing], but when you break it down locally … you'd feel sorry for the children. You'd know them.

The people of Inis Mór have always been open-minded, according to Olwen, a fact confirmed when she and Michael lived together for a year prior to their marriage, during a time when he was teaching at the local school: 'That was in the 1980s. There was a kind of liberalism here.' I contrast the island community's response to them with that of Wexford teacher Eileen Flynn around the same time, 1982 – she lost her job at a convent school because she was living with a separated man. Olwen recalls the case and provides an example of islanders' liberalism by telling me about the community's response to a gay male couple living on Inis Mór. The locals were 'totally accepting' and 'wouldn't have bad-mouthed them or anything, [they were] just seen as different'.

Ireland's successful passage of legislation enabling marriage equality in 2015 was evidence of a growing acceptance of same-sex couples and an acknowledgement of their equal rights in Irish society. The referendum on abortion in 2018 was a more complex issue. Olwen later tells me that she has always agreed with abortion, 'knowing that I would probably never have to have one – a privileged position'. In 2018, when discussing the upcoming referendum on abortion, the reference point for Olwen and her friends was the 'X case' of 1992 when the Irish High Court rescinded the constitutional right to travel of a fourteen-year-old girl who was pregnant as a result of rape because she intended to travel to England to obtain an abortion: 'None of us would want abortion if not necessary, but none of us would stop it.' Another landmark case in 2012 was the death of Savita Halappanavar, an Indian-born dentist living in Ireland who was denied an abortion at Galway University Hospital. Savita died of sepsis. Her death was the catalyst for the 'Repeal the 8th Amendment' movement (the amendment stated that the unborn child had an equal right to life with the mother, effectively banning abortion except when the mother's life was in danger). Savita died because she was refused a medical procedure – an abortion – that would have saved her life. Her case demonstrated the horrific consequences of an institutional response, based on the legal constraints of the time, and the need for reform.

Now aged sixty-three, Olwen tells me that the most significant personal change in her life over the last thirty years, apart from her experience of motherhood, which was profound, was studying for a master's degree later in life.

> It was transformative. Yes, motherhood changes you, but I did a fantastic master's degree when I was about fifty in ecology and religion. Amazing! That changed my thinking. It was just care for the Earth, like learning how much plastic is in the seas. That's only coming out now. The whole role of women and the different waves of feminism. How the Earth has always been treated as female and oppressed. It's taken from the Bible – to be dominated. To control it rather than nurture.

Studying as a mature student enabled Olwen to grow – to learn how to source reliable information that she felt entitled to, could grasp much more easily, and understand. She was also made aware of the double burden placed on women from the 1970s onwards – when more women entered the labour market in Ireland – the ridiculous expectation that women would continue to be responsible for domestic work and childcare too. Now, she thinks men are more centrally involved in the rearing of children and domestic work.

> I do feel that those of us born in the 1960s or late 1950s with free education for women, we went to school, to college, but we were expected to run the home as well. So, you were taking on two jobs. Now men take up the slack as well. They know. It's parenting now, it's not just babysitting.

Knowledge and access to knowledge is vital to being an informed member of any community, any society, especially such a unique community like Inis Mór. According to Olwen, accessing reliable information is about power, about knowing. To illustrate her point, she describes how as a young mother she had to rely on one poorly produced booklet, which was excellent for the time, to inform her about breastfeeding, what she called 'The Hairy Mothers Book' – because of the abysmal drawings of hairy women.

> With the internet you're not relying on anybody. You just go and research it yourself. There's the most amazing knowledge about how breastfeeding works, how it applies to the child, how the breast produces milk responding to the child. Knowledge was power and it was held by the few – the clergy disseminated it and controlled books.

With her children reared and well established in their professional lives, Olwen enjoys her role as grandmother, working part-time during the summer months as a tour guide at Dún Aengus, and getting away with Michael for their annual holiday in Spain.

Olwen Gill, Inis Mór, 2023
PHOTO BY THE AUTHOR

CHAPTER 6

RUTH MELLISH

In the early 1990s, when I first met Ruth Mellish, Belfast city was crippled with violence or the threat of violence, symbolised by the ubiquitous presence of British soldiers at street corners and checkpoints. It was not a place to visit lightly, especially from the Republic, and certainly not by car, because the registration plates would identify your place of origin, and your perceived religion. There had to be a purpose to travel to Belfast in the 1990s. I was careful not to speak in public places in case my accent identified me as someone from the South, and assumptions made about my political affiliation. My trips to Belfast often took place around Brigid's Day, the first day of Imbolc, when I visited a friend, now deceased, who brought us to a pagan healing well by Lough Neagh, to gather rushes to make crosses.

Ruth Mellish (a pseudonym) was then only twenty-three years old. She told me right away that she identified as a feminist and was therefore fascinated by this project, because it concerned the lived experience of various women on the island of Ireland. At that time, she was working at a community centre on a state-sponsored programme, having just finished her degree at Queen's University Belfast. She was biding her time, trying to determine her 'real' professional direction in life. Raised Presbyterian, Ruth's mother encouraged education, considered it vitally important, because her own working-class background had deprived her of that opportunity. The day before Ruth and I met, a bomb exploded in the city's Shaftesbury Square on her way to work. The noise was deafening, glass everywhere. She was shocked but continued on her way. This was not exactly a daily occurrence, though it was not unusual either. As a young woman, Ruth steeled herself for the daily walk to work. There was a war going on. She could be searched by British soldiers at any time. Exploding bombs were a regular and frightening reality.

What struck me most about Ruth then was her feistiness, a spirited, plucky energy that seemed such a contrast to the dourness of the city on a grey day, the bleakness of the Black Mountain dominating my sense of the place. Yes, she was youthful. Just finished university. She could have been downbeat, given that the job she had at the time was a government programme, with minimum wage, a sort of stop-gap position, albeit one with a sense of purpose in a community-based project. As she explained in our first meeting in the 1990s, she had chosen to study psychology because of her desire to learn more about human behaviour.

> I'd done an O-level psychology course with a teacher [at secondary school]. She was enthusiastic, fired with enthusiasm. Since then, I've never really lost that interest. I enjoyed it at Queen's, though I thought that we'd do a lot of the abnormal side – schizophrenia, depression and all that. And I thought I'd come out with a deeper understanding of myself. But it was very behaviouristic in the beginning – why animals do things, like dogs barking. Then the course became more broadly based. We did stuff that was bordering on anthropology, which I really enjoyed as well.

The course lasted three years. Ruth graduated into an environment with few jobs and the 'Troubles' in full force. However, she'd always known her own mind, trusted her own instincts, knew how to turn a challenge into an opportunity.

> When I was at school (1980s), the biggest ambition you could possibly have was to be a nurse or a secretary. I just thought – I'm not going to conform to that. They've no right to tell me

> to do that … I thought about dentistry. The school didn't offer chemistry or physics, both necessary. I was told I could forget about it. End of story. I went to the Tech and did chemistry and after never having touched it at all, I got an O-level in one year, which wasn't bad. I thought, well, I'm not going to lie down under this. I wanted to go to university.

No one else in Ruth's extended family on her mother's side had experienced a university education. Her father's family was a different story. They were 'a pretty upper-middle-class' Protestant family, many of whom went to third level. However, Ruth had little or no contact with her dad or his family from a very early age because her parents had divorced.

> Mum's half of the family are very working class, which we still are, more or less. I was one of three that went to university about the same time. One of us is a doctor now, a doctor of medicine! I can't believe it, the wee fellow I used to beat up when I was a kid is now a doctor delivering babies!

Ruth credits her mother with instilling in her a determination in relation to education, a theme that reverberates in many of the women's narratives in this book.

> My Mum always said, 'I want ye to have an education so you'll not' – she was a cleaner – 'so you'll not have to skivvy like this for the rest of your lives.' My mother was supportive emotionally. She couldn't help me financially. She just couldn't.

I was curious about Ruth's religious background and its impact on her to this point, as a young woman in her early twenties. She was raised Protestant, Presbyterian. In the context of Northern Ireland at the time, this seemed like important information to know in order to understand Ruth's life.

> I've only come to realise quite recently, probably since I came to university, just what's going on in Northern Ireland. I was being brought up by my mother who isn't capable of being malicious towards anybody, so there was no sectarianism or hint of sectarianism in our family. To me the twelfth of July was like Christmas and Easter, everybody celebrated it – a day out to go to the beach or have ice-cream. I thought everybody did it. I haven't been to a twelfth of July parade since I was about sixteen, when I was old enough to make up my own mind and I didn't want to go. I hated watching the parade – the drums were so wild, they used to scare me, especially when I was a small child. I always liked the day out. To me that's all the Protestant tradition is – the twelfth of July and stupid men going out and getting drunk. That to me is what Protestant culture is and I don't want anything to do with it.

After university, Ruth opted for the government-supported position for just one year because she knew the centre and its staff. She'd volunteered there for a few months after graduation, unwilling to live a life on the dole. Ruth was assigned to the role of 'information person' – the one who knew how to deal with computers, with agencies, to ensure that clients could get housing benefits or Department of Health and Social Services (DHSS) supports in relation to issues like domestic violence or abortion. The experience opened her eyes to the differences between services for women in Northern Ireland and those in the Republic.

> There was one poor woman came up from Cork, thought she could get an abortion here in Belfast. She'd come all the way by train and then to be told that there was no way she was getting one in the North either. It was terrible. I just don't know how I would cope with a situation like that …

Still, her job was interesting. She immersed herself wholeheartedly in it so that she could feel a sense of purpose even though the pay meant she was just getting by. She'd grown up understanding the importance of work, was expected to contribute to the family's income once she reached her teenage years. In 1992, she told me:

> I worked every holiday since I was sixteen, except my first year at uni. I was in an ice-cream parlour in a summer resort, ice-cream and candy floss. I did that for two summers. I was a nanny for a summer. I worked in an office, worked in hotel kitchens. This government scheme I'm on now is just a fraction more than the dole, enough to make it worth your while. I wanted to be working. I didn't want to be on the dole because it's a great big hole in your CV. I haven't regretted it. I mean I'm not saying that I totally enjoy the work. I like the people here – there's no backbiting, stuff like that. I'm on ninety-three pounds a week.

In the 1990s, with the election of Mary Robinson as Ireland's first woman president, many women like Ruth seemed unafraid to call themselves feminists, to claim feminism as a framework of analysis for understanding society, so I asked her at the time to explain her understanding of feminism and why it was important to her to openly embrace it.

> I don't think feminism is this strident thing that men always try to portray it. Feminism is about respect for yourself. It's about not letting people – men in particular – patronise you on the basis of your sex. To me that's what feminism is. I resent being patronised. I would not let anybody do it. I haven't come across outright sexism, not at Queen's, because psychology was female dominated – about 90 per cent doing it were female – though the lecturers were 60:40 in the male favour. One of the men in our department is the person who deals with sexual harassment at Queen's. He writes books about the topic. We got guidelines to non-sexist language in our dissertations, and you used it or they would pull you up about it.

Back then (the 1990s), Ruth understood her own rhythm at work, knew what she could manage. She limited her lunchbreaks at the community centre to fifteen minutes, rather than 'sit around doing nothing'. I asked her about her positive work ethic, going above and beyond always, something she admitted to 'having all my life'.

> I've been raised on social security more or less. Well, my mum was always on social security because she's a single parent, has been, since I was six years old. She was on her own from then with a six-year-old and a three-year-old. That experience just makes me totally aware of how women are exploited in the workplace. My mum, even with [government] benefits, had to take shit jobs all the time, which obviously she wasn't supposed to do – cleaning contractors are notorious employers. They pay their workers really badly. I mean my mum was working for about one pound an hour! That was ridiculous. She was working right up to last year [1991] and she's still only on about one pound fifty an hour [as a cleaner]. I'm getting double what she's getting an hour. She knew the trap she was in and wanted me out of that trap.

With few prospects in Northern Ireland in the early 1990s, Ruth resisted the idea of emigration, not only because it would mean living away from her mother, but also because there was a boyfriend on the scene, someone she wanted more time with to see where it might lead. She told me back then:

> If I did think of emigrating, it would be to Britain. It wouldn't be further afield. I couldn't see us going to America or Australia [Ruth and her boyfriend]. I don't think it would be to England. It would be Scotland or Wales, Scotland probably, because they're more similar to us.

Further education, graduate studies, was the main option Ruth considered as her next step. She'd applied for and was awaiting a response to her application to a master's programme in psychology at Queen's. The idea of studying again was appealing to her because if she managed to secure a place on the course – limited to just a few applicants – she'd automatically receive a full grant. In her day-to-day routine, while working at the community centre, she was drawn to taking courses anyway, going to seminars in what were considered the more cutting-edge topics like computers and information technology. Given the limited range of options in terms of her next career step, she seemed to be considering each one carefully, sensing if it was the right fit for her.

> I've always been good at that, reading myself and other people well. That was because of the way I was brought up and the situation I was in. I had to know what sort of mood a person was in, how they were going to react to things. I suppose it's something I've acquired. So, I am an empathetic person. I probably acquired that too, though I'd say there's a certain amount of that that you're born with. Maybe.

In 1992, Belfast remained the most attractive place for Ruth to live, despite the 'Troubles'. I asked her about its impact on her day-to-day life, if the presence of armed soldiers and tanks ever faded into the background, if she ceased to think about the fact that Belfast was located in a warzone.

> It's my home even though this week I was coming down to work and the whole route down to work was just broken glass. The whole way down! There was a bomb in Shaftesbury Square. They'd cordoned off my usual route. You never cease to see the soldiers. I mean somebody pointing a gun at you, you know they're pointing a gun at you – I would always notice that! I don't particularly like it either. It does affect you on the way to work and at work everyone will come in and go, 'Did you see that?' and 'Isn't it terrible.' But that's the end to it. You go on. We're a totally non-sectarian organisation. If a conversation like

> that got started it would get stopped very soon. We don't discuss it really. If I started to get intimidated or something, that would be totally different, but up to now it hasn't [happened].

With no end to the 'Troubles' in sight, I wondered how Ruth thought about the violence and what it might take to end it.

> The solution? It would just be so nice. If everybody started to think about what the other side have to be bitter about, then everybody might appreciate a bit more about what's happening. You might have a bit more sympathy and understanding about the other side and why they think what they do, but unfortunately, that's still not likely to happen.

I remarked that her response, her solution, was based on empathy, something she'd been highly attuned to from an early age. 'Yea, that's what I'm doing. To think a little bit more, everybody, before they go out and shoot someone.'

I asked about her experience of the Irish Republic, and her impression of life south of the border.

> I think of control, church control, and it's not much better up here. The Free Presbyterians aren't in favour of abortion or divorce either. It's the only time you'd get Paisley [Rev. Ian Paisley] and a priest on the same platform is over a women thing that affects women's rights like abortion or divorce. The collars have more in common than they'd ever admit. I've no time for them at all, which is why I said I've no religion. I just don't want to be associated with it.

In the summer of 2023, I board a brand new, comfortable train from Connolly Station in Dublin, heading to Belfast. All around me are passengers speaking in various languages, tourists, I expect, drawn up north to see the sights – the impressive Titanic Museum and the colourful paramilitary murals in certain communities. Many tourist attractions have been developed to ensure the city is attractive and accessible to visitors – one of the many peace process dividends. In fact, Belfast is one of the main tourist destinations for visitors to the island of Ireland, including massive cruise ships that berth at Stormont Wharf in the city's harbour. On this bright summer's day, I encounter a beautiful city despite its association with the political violence of the 'Troubles'. At Queen's University, where US politician Hillary Clinton is now chancellor, there's a new statue of former US Senator George Mitchell, the man who worked tirelessly to broker the Good Friday/Belfast Peace Agreement 1995, signed into law in 1998.[1]

On my way to meet Ruth again after thirty years, the streets of Belfast are undoubtedly safer than they were in the early 1990s – there are no soldiers present. The peace agreement, twenty-five years old in 2023 and still holding, has silenced the guns and bombs.[2] However, political division remains. In June 2023, Northern Ireland is without a functioning government. The devolved government and executive which have power over the region collapsed in January 2017 over disagreements between the Democratic Unionist Party (DUP) and Sinn Féin (the republican party). Attempts by many interests to restore a power-sharing government have been unsuccessful. In the end, I'm told, the solution may well be a numbers game in terms of the majority population in the six counties in the future. The 2021 census shows Catholics at almost 50 per cent of the population with 43.5 per cent who identify as Protestant. This compares with the 2011 census, where Protestants outnumbered Catholics 48 per cent to 45 per cent. It appears that the Catholics are outbreeding the Protestants, whose ancestors were part of a seventeenth-century plantation of Scottish and English settlers.

There are signs of progress, too. In 1997, the first nationalist was elected mayor of Belfast, Alban Maginness of the Social Democratic and Labour Party (SDLP). Since then, members of the SDLP and Sinn Féin regularly serve as mayor, along with representatives of various unionist parties. However, in a post-Brexit context (the UK voted to leave the EU in a 2016 referendum), and with the UK in political crisis, it's difficult to know the constitutional future of Northern Ireland. The past is always present on the island of Ireland.

The twenty-three-year-old woman I met thirty years ago is a mature woman now in her fifties. Ruth is a well-respected professional, working in the field of education with what she terms a 'digital generation', a job she explains is a direct progression from her graduate studies, undertaken after we'd met in the 1990s. Her clients are young people who prefer to communicate via texting, messaging and online exchanges rather than face-to-face meetings. She describes the current generation of young people she works with as ill-prepared for the real world. They appear awkward during in-person meetings, uneasy even, and lacking social skills. A focus of her work is the area of information and communications technology (ICT) – determining its impact on learning, on people's behaviour – and exploring the potential threats and benefits of artificial intelligence (AI) for learners and the field of education. It's important work she finds interesting, even cutting-edge. 'ChatGPT [an artificial intelligence programme] was released [in November 2022] without anyone really knowing what it might be used for – I just don't trust it.' Students have adopted it, delighted to have a source, however flawed, to short-circuit the research process when preparing papers. The educational institutions are at a loss because ChatGPT is a whole new tool with unforeseen implications for education.

I sense that during this meeting in 2023 Ruth seems more subdued – a measure of age, perhaps, or maybe it's something else. I ask if my sense is correct. She considers my query.

She explains that, although the street violence in Belfast may be no more, the threats to women have gone underground, into the new public space of the internet, especially social media. She tells me that she was 'stalked' by a man for almost a year – a frightening and life-changing experience – before he desisted.

'I'm sure that he found a new target after me and that he's had many before me, too.' As a result, she's unwilling to be identified for this project now. There is an irony in the fact that someone whose work focuses on the internet, on social media, on ICT and AI has decided since that experience to hide her real identity when she's active on the internet and social media platforms. And not only that. Ruth also declines to be photographed for work-related events, avoids certain social situations, and no longer travels by public transport. She has decided that this is how she will live her life. It's a position that reminds me of the words of feminist Jacqueline Rose: 'A lasting injury done by threats of violence is a hijacking of thought.'[2]

While Ruth was deeply unsettled by the 'stalker' and has tailored her life in a particular way because of that experience, it's not the whole of her life. She is keen to add that she's happily married to a Catholic, from the South, someone she met in her 'middle years'.

However, I am struck by what I perceive as her toned-down energy, her earlier feistiness waning, at least from my point of view. Despite an end to the war in Northern Ireland, there has been a documented increase in violence against women on the island as a whole. According to a survey conducted in the North in 2023, some 70 per cent of women felt that existing legislation was not effective at tackling online violence against women and girls, and some 85 per cent supported making online violence a criminal offence. In September 2023, the Irish Republic's minister for justice, Helen McEntee, received government approval to establish a new domestic, sexual and gender-based violence (DSGBV) agency. Also in 2023, the National Women's Council in the Republic declared that violence against women was at 'crisis' levels as one woman a week had died in violent circumstances from the start of the year. These developments and Ruth's experience raise serious questions: When and how did things escalate to this degree whereby women's lives are so at risk of violence on the island of Ireland? What will it take for governments – north and south – to effectively regulate social media platforms, which represent the new public space in society, given the documented risks? Ireland has advanced on so many levels – how do we make sense of this escalating unsafe climate for women within society? I ask Ruth to give her perspective, based on her experience in Northern Ireland.

> The prejudice is still there. There is a generational shift in behaviour. If someone doesn't agree with you, they make complaints to the authorities and won't stop. And now there are refugees in Belfast – from Afghanistan, Syria, Iran and the Ukrainians – they are here for work, to make a new life for their families. I voted for Brexit, to leave the EU, because I saw it as undemocratic and corrupt. It started out with a good purpose. Now it's undemocratic. Look what happened in 2008 – they backed the bankers, not the people. That tells you enough.

Asked about the possibility of a united Ireland in her lifetime, Ruth laughs out loud.

> The South has come a long way – with social legislation and lots of other things. It's still a Catholic hegemony and that frightens Protestants. Politicians pay lip service to inclusion. The economic argument is still there, though: can the South afford us? I don't think so.

She and her husband spend holidays hiking down south, so her perspective is informed by her many visits there, albeit to mostly rural areas. She seeks solace in the beauty of the outdoors, in the mountains, a blessed relief from the research she is expected to engage with regarding social media trends and its impact on students.

> It's not that old [social media] when you think about it [2004 Facebook/Meta, 2005 YouTube, 2006 Twitter]. The behaviour!

> There are platforms where people give and take offence, where sexual commentary and sexual conduct of the most vile nature is promoted. It's cyberbullying, misinformation, disinformation and hatred for the most part. That wasn't what it was supposed to be. There's a fascism to it. The mental health consequences for young people are enormous, and of course there's the loneliness. Posting polarising arguments is its engine – it's fuelling its own life. Points of view are dismissed, attacked. People are silenced. It's not real debate. It's not meant to be. In many ways, we're going backwards – equality was unremarkable. If you don't agree with me, there will be consequences. Frightening. I'm horrified by what I see.

Ruth reminds me that while her work requires her to conduct research in this area, she navigates the online world using an alias, a conscious decision on her part, to protect herself and not just because of her experience of being stalked some years ago. Her concept of safety in society has been radically altered. She's also careful in public places and never uses public transportation.

I sense that she's simply had enough, and it's understandable, given the negative forces operating in the new social world online. This was not what she anticipated as the focus of her work following postgraduate studies. It's what she's been called on to do. As she walks me to the exit at her place of work, she tells me that she is seriously considering early retirement even though she is only fifty-four years of age. Life is too short. There are too many fine hikes she has yet to walk. Being in nature is where she wants to be, not monitoring the online madness from an office in Belfast city.

As I sit in my comfortable seat on the slick, modern train back to Dublin, I find myself terribly upset, angry at the fact that while so many people from many different nations worked collectively for so long to ensure peace in Northern Ireland, what has replaced the guns and the bombs is an online warzone extending way beyond this area, a fact that appears to be ignored by those in power, with extremely damaging consequences for young people, the next generation, and especially women. Ruth's feistiness has waned, replaced, in my view, by a caution informed by evidence, a vigilance, a curtailing of exchanges in her own society, all with a view to her personal safety, survival and quality of life.

CHAPTER 7

PATRICIA HAMILTON

On 10 March 2017, a recording of a live BBC television interview conducted via video chat with Professor Robert Kelly went viral because during the discussion on politics in South Korea, two children enter the room – one a toddler, the other in a rolling baby walker. He continues the discussion while pushing back the toddler with one arm. A woman rushes in, grabs the two children and removes them as fast as she can from the room. The video has been viewed over 9 million times. People still find it amusing. Two things struck me about the responses to the video on social media. One was that people assumed that the Asian woman in the recording was the children's nanny. In fact, she is their mother, but it's true that Asian women, especially Filipino women, have established a niche as care workers globally, often leaving their own children behind in the home country to earn income abroad. Second, the man, Professor Kelly, sought to push his children away, a sign that they were not his responsibility, at least not at that time.

Sociologist Arlie Russell Hochschild argues that caring work – childcare and eldercare – is perceived as having low value in western societies despite the essential need for it and the demanding nature of the work. Her solution is to raise the value of care by involving fathers in the care of family members worldwide, so that carework would 'spread laterally instead of being passed down a social class ladder'.[1] Since it is men who have for the most part 'stepped aside from care work', she cites Norway as the model to which we should aspire because all employed men there are eligible for a year's paternity leave at 90 per cent salary.

In many respects, what happened in the recording with the Kelly family in South Korea was a precursor of what unfolded during COVID when many people with children were forced to work from home because of the pandemic. What we now know is that during the pandemic most households assumed traditional gender roles in terms of childcare and domestic labour, including households in Ireland. How a society views and responds to the issue of childcare matters. Its availability and cost can determine a family's well-being and, indeed, the trajectory of careers, especially for women who wish to work outside the home.

Patricia Hamilton, 2023
PHOTO BY THE AUTHOR

Patricia Hamilton knows all about this experience, having learned how to juggle childcare and a professional life for decades. When we met in 1992, her first child was an infant. While we talked in a hotel lobby, her husband Tom took care of the child in the car because the family was commuting from their home in Ballyvaughan, County Clare, to Galway city daily. In 2023, when we meet again, she tells me they've had five children in total, all of them healthy and well. She couldn't have done it – reared her children and worked full-time – without the cooperation of an employer who agreed to her working on flexible terms when necessary and, crucially, the help of another woman whom she paid to mind the children. In addition, her choices regarding work and children were also facilitated by her husband: 'I was lucky I had the security of Tom. I had the security of knowing that we could manage financially.' Patricia's family could afford to pay for childcare. However, many families struggle to do so because even with government subsidies, it's not cheap, never has been, unless of course it's provided by extended family members, usually for free. Increasingly in Ireland, because of the financial strain on young families, elderly parents are being called upon to step up to the task, parenting again in their seventies and eighties, if they are willing, able and live nearby.

Patricia worked as a national school teacher for five years before deciding she wanted to study law. She successfully made inroads into the legal profession, without the usual family connection which can be vital to securing work as a solicitor, while also bearing and rearing five children. Her years working in her chosen career have been intense, extremely challenging, albeit satisfying, mostly because of her desire to combine it with having children. Her experience as a professional woman who wanted to continue to work and have a family is illustrative of the pressures that can be brought to bear on working families in the absence of a free state-supported childcare infrastructure to support them.

At our first meeting three decades ago, I ask Patricia to tell me about her family of origin, the Hamiltons in Sligo:

> My original family had six children. I was the fourth. My father was a psychiatric nurse. My mother was also a nurse before she got married. She gave up after that and never went back into the workforce.

I ask her to define the family's social class because I see it as a relevant question at this point even though I rarely ask this question directly. Instead, I prefer to let the information emerge from a woman's narrative. However, I assume that the legal profession is dominated by people of middle-class origin – at least in the 1990s – and I want to test this assumption. People may define their social class by the family they're born into, but education and work can offer social mobility and therefore put them in another social class in their adult lives. In this case, Patricia is clear:

> In terms of class I would say comfortable working class. We lived in a council house [public housing] in Sligo where education was a priority. Our house was in the most beautiful place, by the river, absolutely gorgeous. It was a most unusual place in that almost everybody in it [the estate] were originally from the country, so it was a very grounded kind of place. Very solid, sound, nice people.

Patricia tells me that her education followed a typical route from the local primary school in Sligo town to secondary school with the Mercy Sisters. At the convent school she received a strong message that as a young girl she wasn't to excel, even though she was bright:

> The nuns looked upon confidence badly, or if you did well, it was showing off. This was drilled into me. It is a very peculiar attitude which has taken me years to shake off. I drew as little attention to myself as possible. That was my aim. I had a grand easy passage through secondary school. I was a desperate idler, but even so, I got five honours in the Leaving Cert.

She is extremely critical of the lack of advice available to her as a young woman deciding on a career direction.

> We had a nun who had probably done some course [in career guidance], but she basically gave us all these aptitude tests and then ignored the results completely – and what you said, what you said you'd like to do. I remember toying with the idea of engineering without much of an idea of what it was, in fairness.

> She just scoffed and said, 'Oh, you have to have honours maths for that.'

The convent did not offer honours maths. One of Patricia's sisters was teaching, and she encouraged her to consider it. 'I went teaching. It was more something I drifted into rather than anything else.'

Her parents were delighted that Patricia was going to be a teacher. They valued education – highly – because of their own limited experience of it. Her father never progressed past primary school. Her mother attended secondary for just a couple of years. For Patricia, however, the training college in Dublin was unsatisfactory, 'monotonous, very restricting, very unstimulating'. She would have preferred a university education but played it safe, hid her true intellectual ability. 'I was just getting through on as little as possible.' Following her training, she took a job in Dublin and then secured a permanent position in her hometown of Sligo, where she taught for almost five years.

> I never made a conscious decision to teach. I was pretty sure I didn't want to teach for the rest of my life. It's not to say that I was actively unhappy at what I was doing. I wasn't stimulated. I can't say I ever loved teaching.

Patricia was twenty-five when she decided to make a switch from teaching and to study law instead, with the aim of practising as a solicitor. She remembers that her father's reaction was to support her decision to give up teaching, but knowing that she was extremely bright, he advised her to study accounting or some other profession where she could succeed purely on merit, not based on family or social connections to 'get a toe in'. He was attuned to the privileges of social class networks and connections.

> They both were highly intelligent people who never had the opportunity of education. Both psychiatric nurses. My mother had a bit of secondary school education. My father had none.

> But they were really well read. They could hold their own anywhere in conversation. In latter years, they both went back and did some kind of diploma in UCG. They valued education really highly.

As a result of her parents' encouragement, Patricia's siblings are all well-educated professionals. All graduated from third-level institutions with qualifications ranging from a diploma to a PhD. Her eldest sister was an accountant, her second sister has a PhD in psychology. Her three brothers studied construction, engineering and marketing and all have high-powered jobs in various parts of the world – the Middle East, the UK and the USA.

In the 1980s, when Patricia wanted to switch profession from teaching to the law, she availed of a government scheme offering leave of absence from state jobs. She applied for a year off without losing her permanent teaching position. That lessened the risk. 'I went to Rathmines [in Dublin] to study law.' Her choice was influenced by a friend whose husband was studying law – she reckoned that Patricia would love it. Her friend was right! 'At the end of the year in Rathmines, I studied for the summer and did the exam for the Law Society in November.' She passed with flying colours. However, for the next step in her legal training she had to secure 2,500 pounds in fees by September of the following year. She returned to substitute teaching to gather the necessary funds. Meanwhile, she and Tom decided to get married during the summer before her course began.

At that time, in the mid-1980s, a person with a university degree or experience as a law clerk could apply to take the exam at the Law Society. Training as a solicitor entailed a combination of blocks of courses at the Law Society, Blackhall Place in Dublin, and a period of apprenticeship with a firm of solicitors. A condition of acceptance onto the course at the Law Society was an assurance of a place with a firm of solicitors willing to take on Patricia as an apprentice. That was not an easy ask, since she had no relatives or friends practising law.

> I think it is more difficult for people from my family background to gain entrance to the profession. So many of my class at the Law Society came from family firms, had connections with other professionals. Their fathers were connected with someone who had a family firm. It is difficult to break in if you haven't some kind of connection with the law or at least with business. Before I could start the course, I had to find myself a law firm to have my indentures signed. I had to be apprenticed to a master who signed my indentures. This [apprenticeship] lasts three years. It was very hard to break into a law firm.

Patricia realised that not only were there social class networks operating that provided an unfair advantage to those training for a career in law, but there were also financial obstacles to obtaining a foothold in the profession.

> You must pay about 200 pounds when you sign your indentures. Then you must live in Dublin for six months. The advanced course which I did was 700 or 800 pounds. This after you've done a degree. It's a lot of money. The recommended Law Society salary for an apprentice is 85 pounds a week, or was when I was getting my apprenticeship. It would be difficult for people from a one-salary family, regardless of class ... to put their child through four years of college and then find 2,000 or 2,500 pounds and then expect their son or daughter to live [during the apprenticeship] on 85 pounds a week.

At this stage, Tom had qualified as a civil engineer and was working in a full-time job in Galway city. His support was a crucial factor in enabling Patricia to become a solicitor. Without his encouragement and financial support, it would not have been possible. He knew how smart she was, and at that point in their lives wanted her to realise her potential.

> In fact, at that stage [1992] he'd probably encourage me to go further [in her studies generally, not just the law]. I don't have

> any desire to study for the bar, but if I did, I don't think I'd have a hope of breaking into it. You would want to have a fair bit of money behind you to spend a few years devilling [apprentice to a barrister]. Then as a junior counsel you are depending on solicitors to give you briefs. Whatever hope you have as a solicitor with no connections, you have none as a barrister. It is very tough.

Ever the realist, Patricia persevered and eventually found a firm of solicitors in Galway city willing to take her on as an apprentice.

> More often than not, you have to find a new firm [to employ you] when the indentures run out. Some of the larger firms give you a contract for a year after you qualify, and then when you have a year's experience you are in a better position to sell yourself. Others have a policy of always having an apprentice in the firm, so when one's indentures run out, they have another apprentice in the firm.

Her graduation as a fully fledged solicitor at that firm coincided with her first pregnancy. There was no obligation on her employer to keep her now that she was finished her indentures. Having demonstrated her abilities, however, she was offered a permanent position at the firm once she qualified. It was an anxious time as she was starting out in this new professional career – how would the employer respond to news of the pregnancy and her need to go on maternity leave? Would the job offer still hold?

> If he [the owner of the legal practice] had wanted to, he would have had no difficulty in saying goodbye [after the period of indentures]. He would be perfectly legally entitled to do so. But not only did he keep me on, he negotiated a four-day week with me. My boss's attitude was very positive to this arrangement.

Indeed, such an attitude coming from an employer was unusual for the time, the early 1990s, so I ask her to explain why she thinks he was so amenable to the arrangement.

> He had three kids of his own. He's never given any trouble with time off. He's very flexible about everything. He has lots of management skills and in that way he and the firm see the benefit in that [being flexible with employees]. The reason for working the four-day week was mainly because of the baby, Joe, but I think it's a wonderful idea. I didn't want to work a five-day week, nine to six, away from him.

Patricia was pleased that her job now suited her need to combine work for income – work that was stimulating, that interested her – with her desire to be a mother and to have children.

> It needn't be a problem for women who choose to work [for income] and have children at the same time. The job can lend itself to that kind of flexibility, if the employers have a flexible attitude. That is what counts ultimately.

Having successfully negotiated a four-day week with her employer once her first child was born, she was still expected to put in a full day at the office on those days, 9 a.m. to 6 p.m., then face the commute back to Ballyvaughan, County Clare, an hour's car journey from Galway city. Once she found a suitable, willing childminder in Galway, she and Tom had to review their circumstances – again. With each of them putting in long workdays, driving the hour's commute to and from work, dropping off and collecting the child, something had to give. Eventually, the family decided to relocate to Galway city.

It was not an easy task for women to source suitable childcare support at that time in Ireland. From the early 1990s, Irish women entered the labour market in large numbers. There wasn't a sufficient supply of childcare workers to meet the increased demand, and so the cost soared. Many families who already required two incomes to pay a mortgage struggled to meet the childcare costs. Of course, the irony is that care work – whether eldercare or childcare – was then and is now predominantly work taken up by women. Ideally, the state should play a central role and the Irish state offered schemes in support of childcare, including tax credits and so forth, a recognition of the extent of the financial burden on Irish families. At the same time, European Union programmes aimed at supporting women's greater participation in the labour force in the 1990s encouraged new approaches by community-based organisations to develop suitable childcare in their areas. For example, one of the organisations I worked with at the time, Doras Buí, a community organisation on the northside of Dublin with vast experience in the area of childcare, successfully devised, developed and provided guaranteed accredited childcare training for its participants based on international best practice.

By 2003, Ireland was ranked the most globalised nation of sixty-two countries by *Foreign Affairs* magazine, because of its trade, multinational investment and ICT, according to a report by Cliff Taylor in *The Irish Times* (8 January 2003). Mirroring the pattern operating in globalised nations, from the 2000s onwards, as new migrants arrived in greater numbers, migrant women assumed the care-work role in twenty-first-century Ireland. For example, at the Migrant Rights Centre Ireland, located in Dublin, migrant women – often from Eastern Europe, the Philippines and Africa – were supported to collectively organise as a domestic workers group. As the group built its capacity, the women sought the protection of the trade union movement for decent terms and conditions as members of SIPTU (Services Industrial Professional and Technical Union).

In June 2023, just over thirty years after our initial conversation, Patricia tells me that in advance of our meeting, she's been thinking a lot about childcare and maternity leave. The terms of statutory maternity leave have improved considerably in Ireland since she first availed of them, a change that was necessary, she believes, based on her experience with her first child, Joe.

> Looking back, one of the things that has really struck me was thank goodness for maternity leave. Mothers are off now for ages [twenty-six weeks of maternity leave]. When Joe was born on the seventeenth of October I was back at work after Christmas. Not only that, I had been sick. I was back in hospital a week after he was born with an infection. I was so sick. That medical time, back in the hospital, was just lost in the middle of my maternity leave. Looking back, I was a wreck when I went back to work.

Patricia might have asked for additional time off as sick leave on top of the statutory maternity leave available at that time, but she had only recently qualified as a solicitor and her employer was already accommodating her by agreeing to let her work a four-day week. She wanted to keep her job. And she didn't want to push her luck. 'I was so busy [at work] and so grateful to have a job at the time that I went back after Christmas.'

Thankfully, Ireland has improved its maternity leave provisions since Patricia first availed of them. In the 1990s, based on submission of a medical certificate to her employer confirming her pregnancy, Patricia was entitled to fourteen weeks' leave under the terms of the 1981 Maternity Protection of Employees Act. Entitlements were improved under the Maternity Protection Act, 1994 and later the Maternity Protection (Amendment) Act, 2004. The current entitlement is to twenty-six weeks' maternity leave together with sixteen weeks' additional unpaid maternity leave. Now, a woman may take this time off work from full-time, casual or part-time employment. A Parental Leave Act was introduced in 1998 for employees who are the natural or adoptive parent of a child, offering fourteen working weeks' leave to care for the child.

In retrospect, she tells me that not only did she return to work too early after the birth of her first child when she was still fighting an infection, she was also emotionally distressed leaving her baby. She remembers the emotional strain and the practicalities required to ensure she could breastfeed her infant, which she was determined to do.

> I was heartbroken leaving the baby. He was probably fine. I was breastfeeding him. I used drive from Ballyvaughan [County Clare], leave him at the babyminder's [in Galway] in the morning and feed him. Go into the office. I'd go out on my lunch break and feed him again. I expressed milk as well, for the in-between times. Then back out in the evening to collect him and feed him again. It was really, really tough.

Despite the challenges, she and Tom decided to have their children in quick succession, while they were healthy and young. Joe, their first, was born in October 1991. Then a daughter Claire in 1994. In 1997, they had twin boys, Peter and Tim. Their last child, Grace, was born a year later, in 1998. Therefore, by 1998 they had five children, three of whom were under two years of age.

> By the time I had the fifth child, I was doing work in one section of the office which was personal injuries. The personal injuries stuff was interesting and varied, but it was also out of control timewise. If I had a case coming up, I had to be available all hours of the night and away in Dublin a lot [for court proceedings]. I opted for the stuff that was more controllable, bank work.

Patricia also had to source a different childminder, someone willing to take on three children under the age of two, to mind them in their home or in Patricia's home. She did not want her infant children in a crèche. The person she found had children of her own who were attending secondary school, someone who wanted to be home to mind her own children after school but who was willing to work as a childminder in the mornings. Patricia had to negotiate her work schedule – again.

> I said to my boss – I can work mornings. I have this woman who is able to mind my children. I can't get anybody suitable full-time. I remember him coming up with a suggestion – to go

> to the university and get a rota of people. I said, 'These are my children! I can't have a rota of children minding babies.' It was kind of like a cleaning project for him.

Patricia says that the attitude expressed by her boss, who was already extremely cooperative in relation to her work schedule, demonstrated that he simply didn't get what it takes to mind children, small babies, and it was not an unusual attitude. By way of explanation, she tells me about an encounter at that time with a businessman she was seated beside at a wedding and being asked what she did for a living. She told him:

> 'I'm a solicitor, but I don't know if I will be able to go back [after maternity leave] because there's a problem with childminding.' He said, 'With the internet and everything' – this is in 1998 – 'you could be hooked up and work from home.' I thought, *A man's answer!* I said, 'I don't think you quite heard me. I have no problem working. I could actually go into the office to work. It's finding someone to mind my children.' So, he clearly thought you could just sit there and answer calls from whomever and they [the children] would all just, I don't know, mind themselves or whatever. That suggestion was given to me by one or two other people over the years, all men. No concept.

Patricia's response to the pressures she faced as a young mother, juggling her job with the bearing and rearing of children, reminds me of the fallacy of Sheryl Sandberg's idea, widely promoted in the 2000s, of the need for professional women to just 'lean in', i.e. to accept and take charge of the challenges encountered in the workplace and thereby succeed.[2] The central flaw in this perspective is its focus on changing an individual woman's behaviour rather than ensuring structural change in society in support of families with children and women in the workplace. We can assume that Sandberg's position in upper management at Facebook at the time afforded her sufficient resources to pay for round-the-clock help with her children and domestic work. The central questions that a society must ask, based on Patricia's experience, are: How can we support families with children where both parents work for income?[3] And, within the family home, why is it that women are expected to be primarily responsible for children? Patricia reminds me that one of the positive outcomes of the COVID pandemic when people worked from home was that it dawned on many parents what was involved in trying to do your job while also minding children – the near impossibility of the challenge.

Sociologist Arlie Russell Hochschild argues that in developed societies, with more and more women working for income outside the home, if we want women doctors, bus drivers, teachers, political leaders, plumbers and so forth, we need qualified people to care for the children.[4] In 1944, Ireland introduced a system of children's allowance in support of families. With its reported 8 billion surplus in July 2023, perhaps the Irish state might evaluate and adopt models of best practice in other countries, especially Nordic countries like Finland where the state provides free universal daycare from eight months until the start of formal education at age seven.

In addition to her experience of rearing children while working, Patricia was called upon to care for her ageing, ill mother in Sligo. Increasingly, with Ireland's population living longer than at any time in history, the issue of eldercare has arisen for many families, so Patricia Hamilton was no exception. After her father died, she was travelling up to Sligo every second weekend to visit her mother. Then her mother developed Alzheimer's in 1997, the year Patricia had the twins. With the other siblings scattered around the globe, initially it fell upon the two sisters in Ireland to set up a rota of care for their mother until a more structured residential care situation could be found – no small thing.

> It was 1997, I had just had the twins, so I was on maternity leave. I was already exhausted. I had four small kids. I put them

> in the car [to drive to Sligo]. It was a beautiful day. I clearly wasn't thinking straight because I brought my mother and the kids in the car to the beach. I pulled up at Rosses Point [beach] and realised – I can't mind them! If the toddler runs, I have two in the little carrier. I won't be able to run if one of them dashes. What if my mother decides to make a run for it? I just bought them all ice creams and took them home – crying. It was just awful. I had no idea what I was doing through those years. It was really, really tough. I was just coasting. I wasn't managing. As a family, we [her siblings] found a place for my mother in Dublin, beside my sister.

With her mother's eldercare sorted and once her children were of school-going age, the pressure on Patricia decreased, but she was still full-on parenting, driving them here, there and everywhere for sports and clubs and so forth right through secondary school, and even during their college years too. However, in 2014 everything came to a stop for her when her beloved eldest sister Maura died at the age of sixty-two in Australia. She felt emotionally unmoored. That death was the catalyst for Patricia's radical re-evaluation of everything – a process of deep reflection on her own life, its purpose, its value, its direction. Having reared five children while simultaneously maintaining a professional life for decades, she decided she'd done enough.

> I remember when she died thinking that if I was about to die, what would I say about my life? I have worked! I worked and I have five kids. Do you know what? I don't want to be coming to the end of my days and saying, 'I have worked!' I just want to do nothing. I have the house full of books I want to read. A whole load of things I want to do that involve absolutely nothing.

She now spends her days reading, swimming in the ocean, travelling. She heads down to Ballyvaughan regularly, and travels

Patricia Hamilton celebrating her sixtieth birthday with her family, all dressed in 1960s gear. Front, left to right: Claire, Patricia, Grace. Back, left to right: Tim, Tom, Peter, Joe
PHOTO PROVIDED BY PATRICIA HAMILTON

to Italy – a place she has come to know well – often with one of her children to accompany her, with a stack of books she's always wanted to read.

Based on her experience, Patricia believes accessible childcare and extended maternity and paternity leave are vital in a modern society if families are to thrive. There are many and varied options for Ireland to consider. Also, with remote working now expected to be an option made available to employees following its trial during COVID, the push to return to the workplace will be resisted by those for whom home-based life seems more holistic, unless workplace childcare is made available.

In the 2022 census, the Central Statistics Office introduced a question about childcare for the first time, an indication of its importance as an issue in Irish society. Of those who responded to the question, 331,783 under-fifteen-year-olds said they had attended some kind of childcare. Patricia's home city, Galway, had the highest proportion of children in crèches (57 per cent). Results for other counties in the Republic of Ireland demonstrate that families are availing of a range of childcare options, often with an unpaid relative or family member. In twenty-first-century Ireland, people do what they can to make it work, but it shouldn't have to be this difficult. The solution, based on practice in other countries, is simple – free state-provided childcare for all. Ireland's thriving economy can support such a system.

CHAPTER 8

MARY BANOTTI

'Working for women's rights was an intrinsic part of my life.'

I first met Mary Banotti in Dublin in 1992 at a public meeting organised to discuss the feasibility of forming a women's political party in Ireland. We chatted for a while before she introduced herself as a Dubliner and a member of the European Parliament based in Strasbourg, France. When I explained the aim of this project to her, she agreed to make time for an interview during her few days in Ireland that week. She was open, engaging and totally supportive of the project; she saw value in consulting Irish women about their lives. I remember coming away from that initial encounter thinking that I had not expected such access to a politician nor such candour from an elected European representative. She was fifty-two years old at the time, in the prime

Mary Banotti, 1992
PHOTO PROVIDED BY MARY BANOTTI

of her life, encouraging Irish women at that meeting to have the confidence to 'try their hand at politics'. She shed tears as she spoke of the joy she experienced when her sister Nora was elected to Dáil Éireann in 1981 – 'one of the happiest days of my life'.

When I interviewed Mary Banotti for the first time it was at the European Parliament's offices in Dublin. Just over thirty years later, in 2023, the fiftieth anniversary of Ireland's entry to the EEC/EU, we met at a nursing home in south Dublin. Mary Banotti died in 2024, aged eighty-four, as this book was being finalised.

Many people knew Mary Banotti as the Irish politician with the unusual name, a result of her short-lived marriage to an Italian doctor whom she met while working as a nurse in Africa. She was born into a family that is like political royalty in the Irish context. Her mother, Kitty O'Mahony (née Collins), was the niece of the revolutionary, soldier and politician Michael Collins, one of the delegation that negotiated the terms of the treaty with Great Britain in 1921 that led to the establishment of the Irish Free State in 1922. Kitty experienced 'an extraordinarily traumatic childhood'. Her mother, Mary's granny, died in February 1921. Then the family home near Sam's Cross, Clonakilty in west Cork was burned to the ground by British forces two months later, and Johnny Collins, Kitty's father, was arrested and interned in Spike Island. As Mary Banotti explains in her 2008 book *There's Something About Mary*:

> With her mother dead and their home destroyed, my mother and her seven siblings were split up for a time among various relatives. My mother was among the last to see Michael [Collins] alive when he briefly stopped to visit the family on August 22, 1922 … Two hours later he was dead.

Michael Collins, the commander-in-chief of the national army, was assassinated during the Civil War by anti-treaty IRA forces at Béal na Bláth in west Cork. Fine Gael claim him as one of the main inspirations for its founding as a political party, even though it wasn't established until 1933, after Collins' death. Therefore, Mary Banotti's family has been inextricably linked with the horrors of the Civil War, the formation of the Irish state and the emergence of one of its two major political parties.

Like her legendary relative, Mary Banotti sought to change Irish society based on her experience of living in many different countries and cultures during her lifetime. The focus of Mary's contribution to change was initially within Ireland, through her work as a campaigner for women's equality in marriage, along with feminist Nuala Fennell and others, not party politics. She helped to establish the first safe house for women seeking refuge from domestic violence – a precursor to Women's Aid – and the Rutland Centre, a residential treatment facility to support people dealing with alcohol addiction. The focus of her later political work on behalf of Fine Gael was at European Union level.

Elected as a Fine Gael candidate to the European Parliament in 1984, she successfully represented the Dublin constituency in that role for twenty years, 1984–2004. In 1997, Mary Banotti was selected by the party to contest the presidential election called to replace Mary Robinson, though she lost that election to Mary McAleese. Her younger sister Nora Owen, a prominent member of Fine Gael, won her seat in Dáil Éireann in 1981 and served as minister for justice between 1995 and '97, and deputy leader of Fine Gael from 1993 to 2001.

Mary Banotti carved a path in life and in politics without the support of a partner – she was separated from her husband in 1970, after a brief marriage – and with the responsibility of raising a young daughter. As a parent raising a child alone, she knew she would encounter challenges, but this was not new territory for her. As the eldest in a family of six, she'd witnessed the issues that her widowed mother faced daily. Her mother demonstrated how you roll up your sleeves, get on with life, make it work.

> There were six of us [five girls and one boy]. I'm the eldest of a northside family. We lived in Cabra and then moved to Clontarf.

> Our neighbours would have been middle management, teachers, garda officers. My father was a bank manager. He died when I was ten.

After her father's death, Mary's mother became the family's main breadwinner at age thirty-eight. Originally trained as a teacher of domestic science, she began teaching again at the College of Domestic Science, Cathal Brugha Street in Dublin. Unable to find someone to mind the six children, she first sent Mary and then all her siblings to boarding school.

> My mother believed that education was the only thing she could give me. All of my aunts were educated to work, so I came from a tradition of that. With six children and a job, my mother really couldn't cope, so I went because it was the thing to do and it was supposed to be a good education. The rest of my sisters followed fairly quickly.

At the Dominican convent in Wicklow, where she was a boarder, the young Mary O'Mahony was expected to make the best of the educational opportunity, to get on with it. When I enquired (during our first interview) about her thoughts then, as an adolescent, about what work she'd like to do in the world once she finished school, she told me that her position in the family, the eldest, and their family's circumstances at the time, had a major impact on her choices.

> I was the eldest, and because I hated being dependent on my mother, I did a secretarial course and went into the bank. I hated that and within three days I knew I would have to leave it. I then went to London to become a nurse. At that stage, as the daughter of a widow and having a good job in the bank, it just seemed extraordinarily ungrateful and silly of me to leave a good job like that. I could not be dependent on her. I could not but be aware of how hard she was working, but equally, I

> couldn't bear to have to ask her for everything. So, while I was no longer able to contribute to the family, I wasn't a charge on the family either.

This initial emigration to London was the first relocation of many during years Mary spent living and working abroad, when she also acquired a qualification as a social worker. Her training as a nurse enabled her to get jobs in various places, including Canada and New York, and as a development aid worker in Kenya. In 1967, she moved to Italy, where she married Giovanni Banotti, an Italian doctor she'd met during her time nursing in Africa. Their child Tania was born in Italy.

> I always wanted to tour the world – I don't know why. From the time I was about six, I had this feeling. I felt there was something outside Ireland that was for me. What has characterised a lot of my whole life was the total lack of any clear plan, but what has equally characterised it is that whenever an interesting opportunity arrived, I recognised it as such, and took it.

When we met in 1992, Mary was still legally married – even though her 1967 marriage had lasted a little over a year – because divorce was simply not available in Ireland. What she describes as her own 'traumatic experiences with marital breakdown' were to be a crucial factor in her campaigning work in Ireland during the 1970s. 'Soon after my daughter was born in Rome, my marriage ended, and Tania was abducted [by Mary's husband].' Her baby was returned to Mary after two weeks, at which point she decided they would move back to Ireland. She and Tania arrived in the country in October 1970, three years before it officially joined the European Economic Community, the precursor to the European Union, the institution where she would ultimately work for twenty years.

Those initial years back home in Ireland were difficult. She was not only adjusting to being 'home' again, but she also needed to find work and someone to care for Tania.

> She was very small. My marriage broke up when she was only one and a half. I had to go out and work. The first year I worked as a domestic in a hotel in County Cavan so that I could have her [Tania] with me. That was until she was two and a half and I took that job specifically because I looked into what it would cost for childcare and I found that I would probably be paying 90 per cent of my salary. I thought that was ludicrous and I took a much lower-paying job, but I was allowed to have her with me. So that served two purposes. She needed me and I needed her.

During her time living and working in rural Cavan, she 'formed the first rural branch of the Irish Women's Liberation'. However, as a lone parent in 1970s Ireland, Mary knew her options in terms of work, accommodation and childcare were extremely limited. In 1972, she got a job at Irish Distillers, suppliers and producers of spirits and wine, where she was asked to set up their employee welfare system. That experience opened her eyes to the issue of what she called 'problem drinking'. Her job eventually led her to being asked to host a programme on social welfare information on RTÉ television, the national television station, a programme that successfully ran from 1980 to '84. She stayed working with Irish Distillers for the next twelve years until her election as a public representative.

> Because it was the distilling industry, there was a lot of problem drinking. I became aware of the wholly inadequate systems of treatment for alcoholism available in Ireland at the time and the massive amount of ambivalence and mythology that surrounded it – the denial! I became involved in setting up the Rutland Centre which became the first treatment centre looking at alternative methods of treating alcoholism that included treatment of the family. I was chair of the centre until very recently [she reports in 1992]. It's one of the things I'm happiest at having been involved with over the years.

She also channelled her energies into the women's movement, which was thriving in Ireland in the 1970s, driven by the work of the Irish Women's Liberation Movement. She connected with other feminists such as Nuala Fennell who established AIM (Action, Information, Motivation), an organisation seeking family law reform in Ireland, a topic Mary was deeply interested in. According to the *Dictionary of Irish Biography*, Nuala Fennell also established a group advocating on behalf of deserted wives, ADAPT (Association for Deserted and Alone Parents).[1] As Mary Banotti explains:

> I now found myself in a situation where the focus of the AIM movement was family law, an area that really needed to be changed. I had both a personal, in terms of my own very traumatic experiences with marital breakdown, and a political interest in it. So, that became all-absorbing for the next four or five years.

Their campaigning had impact. Following the general election in 1973, the Fine Gael and Labour coalition government enacted some key pieces of reform sought by AIM and ADAPT – payment of the children's allowance to mothers rather than fathers and a reduction in the time women had to wait to receive the deserted wives allowance, a social welfare support.

In 1974, following the screening of a BBC documentary on domestic violence, *Scream Quietly or the Neighbours Will Hear*, describing Erin Pizzey's establishment of a women's aid centre in London, Mary Banotti travelled with Nuala Fennell to learn more about the centre. In the documentary, two Irish women described their need to flee Ireland with their children to escape violent husbands. Mary and Nuala were determined to provide some protection for women in such circumstances in Ireland. In 1975, the first refuge for women seeking protection from domestic violence was established in Harcourt Street. This was the beginning of the organisation known as Women's Aid, now a leading campaigning and advocacy organisation working on the issue of domestic violence and the trafficking of women.

Prior to her immersion in campaigning work, Mary had joined the local branch of Fine Gael in 1973, 'largely because I felt Fianna Fáil were making such a terrible mess of whatever they were doing then, that I wanted to get involved'. Ten days after she joined Fine Gael, a general election was called, and Mary was thrown into the rough and tumble of an election campaign. Initially, she felt politically naïve:

> I can't say I had the remotest idea what they were about in political terms. I just knew they [Fine Gael] were different to Fianna Fáil at that stage. Fine Gael won the election and went into coalition. I quickly discovered that, really, I had very little in common with the leadership of Fine Gael then, which was very conservative.

In the early 1980s, Mary increased her profile with the Irish public through her work hosting the RTÉ television programme dealing with social welfare issues. She was also viewed with new interest within the ranks of Fine Gael, a party now under the leadership of Garret FitzGerald: 'I was a great admirer of Garret.' However, her earlier experience with the party in 1973 still rankled with her, when her local branch nominated her to represent them at a convention to select candidates to run in the general election.

> I went to the convention and of course I didn't get it [nomination in 1973]. The sitting member of that time was a man I had no respect for and I felt that, with my hands [tied] behind my back, I could do a better job than him. This man came up to me and he said to me in a manner which was both tired and emotional, 'Don't get disappointed,' and I said, 'I'm not disappointed at all, but I am going to take your seat off you.' He didn't even hear me. I tell the story against myself, because I ran for the Senate subsequently (1982/3). He was on the same Senate panel and

> once again he got selected and I didn't and that was ten years later.

I am curious as to why Mary considers this a significant experience to relay, and why it stays with her as an important lesson about women and Irish politics.

> I do know that at the time [1973] – it was reported to me later – some of the older members of the party in the area, you know, ordinary rank and file members, when they realised that I was separated from my husband, they nearly went into orbit at the thought that I might have actually been on the ticket. So in fact there was an instinctive feeling, which I recognised, that as someone who was separated, I hadn't a chance for many years to come.

In a by-election in Dublin Central in 1983, she was again unsuccessful in getting selected to represent the party, but she felt she'd performed well during various media exchanges. The party leadership, and Garret FitzGerald in particular, were of the same view. Within six months of this election, she won her seat at the European Parliament in 1984 and became an MEP: 'By the time I did run, [being a separated woman] was no longer an issue. I also suspect it was a safer bet for the party to have a separated woman representing the Fine Gael party in Europe.'

At our meeting in 1992, I ask her to describe her work as an MEP at that point in her career:

> My present occupation is politics. It's political in the formal sense, in so far as I am a member of a political party, Fine Gael, and I'm a member of a political group [Christian Democrats] in the European Parliament.

Invariably, she'd work a six-day week and sometimes seven. During one week of each month, she spent five days working at the parliament, attending to responsibilities arising from the various committees she served on. Based on the information Mary provided at that time, 1992, the European Parliament was one of four major institutions of the European Community, each with its own role. The European Parliament represented the voters of Europe, and ensured their say in European affairs. The Commission had seventeen independent members, making proposals for legislation and policy; The Court of Justice, interpreting Community law; and an Economic and Social Committee, where economic interest groups advised on European legislation. There was also a Court of Auditors to check the management of the Community's funds and a European Investment Bank.[2]

The work of the European Parliament was conducted in various committees, of which there were eighteen at the time, each dealing with a particular area: political affairs, industrial policy, environment, rules and procedures, etc. Mary was one of 4 Irish members of the 121 Christian Democrats grouping, the second largest political grouping within the parliament in 1992. Her committee work was intense and her trips back and forth to Ireland were far from rest periods. While in Ireland, she was expected to go on school visits to explain her work in the parliament, attend party meetings, work in the EU office, and often work in the Dáil.

> But I enjoy the work, and it energises me. I find that my ability to manage has improved considerably … [also] my confidence – to just assume that I will be able to manage … to go in and do it!

She proved herself capable as a member of the European Parliament, speaking eloquently in three languages, highlighting the concerns of the Irish people in various committee sessions conducted in relation to her portfolio. For example, in 1992 she was the vice-president of the Youth, Culture, Education, Media and Sport Committee; a member of the Environmental Consumer

Protection and Public Health Committee; and member of the Interparliamentary Delegation to the United States and vice-president of the Intergroup on Consumer Affairs. The welfare of women was always central to her concerns and her work, based on her experience of working in what was then called the 'developing world'. She served as an MEP from 1984 to 2004.

Four years after completing her term as an MEP, Mary Banotti published a book entitled *There's Something About Mary.*[3] It opens with an overview, where she writes about her own life to that point, before presenting annotated interviews she conducted with thirteen women named Mary, all active in Irish politics and various political parties, including Mary O'Rourke, TD, Mary Harney, TD, President Mary McAleese, former president Mary Robinson and Mary Lou McDonald, TD. In the final segment of the book she includes her responses to questions posed by her 'literary guide' and friend John Fanagan. Some interesting nuggets emerge from the interview in relation to her own personal life: her admiration of Garret FitzGerald, her genuine regard for the women politicians in the book, and her first speech at the European Parliament in Strasbourg.

For example, she explains that, in 1980s Ireland, Fine Gael leader Garret FitzGerald was an outlier in party politics – the leader of a conservative party who 'quite genuinely hasn't a single sexist bone in his body … was determined that women were going to be part of whatever was going on in the Party'. In her maiden speech to the European Parliament in 1984, Mary opened her remarks by speaking in the Irish language. That caused consternation in the chamber. The chair, Lady Ellis, a British member of parliament, didn't understand and tried to silence Mary, but Northern Ireland MEP John Hume and several other members came to her defence. She'd made her mark. She told me that on regular flights to Strasbourg, she and Ian Paisley, the unionist MEP from Northern Ireland, often sat side by side, with him reading the Bible, while she prepared for meetings. In Europe, she was most noted for her work in key areas: she pioneered issues relating to environmental policy/climate change, when it was not a mainstream issue, also youth and culture, and took a particular interest in and advocated for children separated from their parents, in cases where one parent had absconded with a child.

Mary Banotti, MEP, with Henry Plumb, president, European Parliament, 1987–9
PHOTO COURTESY OF MARY BANOTTI, N.D.

In 2022, I reached out to Mary's daughter, Tania Banotti, a public figure in her role as director of Creative Ireland. Tania encouraged me to prioritise the meeting with her mother, since Mary was demonstrating some early signs of Alzheimer's disease. I did so, and arranged to visit Mary in January 2023. At a beautiful nursing home in south Dublin, I was told that in addition to Mary Banotti, residents included former Fianna Fáil politician Mary O'Rourke and the journalist Bruce Arnold.

In Mary's private room, photos of her with various family members, political allies, European Parliament colleagues and so forth adorned the shelves. In a prominent position was a recent photo of her daughter Tania with Mary's sister Nora Owen taken in August 2022 at an event to commemorate the centenary of the assassination of Michael Collins at Béal na Bláth.

It's a comfortable room, with its own en suite and must, I imagine, cost a fortune. Mary tells me that her long-term memory is better than her short-term recollections, so I focus on that, reminding her of the details of our conversation three decades ago. She tells me that she's eighty-three. She is in lively spirits initially and genuinely interested in learning more about this project and my life before relaying her memories. She tires after about half an hour and I ask if she'd like to rest on the bed as she's just been out to lunch with a friend. I also offer to return on another day. She insists we continue, and is also happy for me to take her photo (reproduced at the end of the chapter).

I ask her what she thinks of Ireland now, in 2023.

> Huge amount of buildings [especially in Dublin]. Massive development. The population exploded and the infrastructure exploded. Yet, there's a housing crisis. The country has developed but the infrastructure has not kept pace.

The other notable difference for her is the diversity of the population.

> The number of people living here [in Ireland] now that are from abroad – that's a significant change. It's not necessarily just Ireland. These people needed some place to live. Staff here represent it [that demographic change]. I live here now, and the staff and nurses are very nice. There are a number of nurses here from India, waiting to have their qualifications recognised. There isn't a single Irish person working on the staff – maybe at the desk [front desk].

Arriving early for our meeting, I had sat in the foyer of the building and witnessed the support and nursing staff go about their duties, listened to the voices, the accents. The person working at the front desk was the only person I'd meet who was Irish-born. Migrants are vital to the operation of this facility. I was told that some nurses are from a particular part of India where historically the Irish Loreto nuns set up schools and hospitals, Kerala.

I ask if Mary thinks immigrants to Ireland are well treated, if the integration process is going well, given that approximately one in five people living in Ireland was born elsewhere.

> Diversity will be its [Ireland's] strength and its challenge. There's been an extraordinary increase in the numbers [of immigrants]. You see it in the shops, in Marks & Spencer [department store]. The political system and structure [are] not yet reflecting the society. There's a lot of racism too.

According to Ireland's Central Statistics Office, in the twelve months to the end of April 2023 the Irish population rose by 97,600 people, the largest twelve-month increase since 2008, the year of the global financial crash. The arrival of 141,600 immigrants represented a sixteen-year high and this was the second successive twelve-month period where over 100,000 people immigrated to Ireland. Of those immigrants, 29,600 were returning Irish citizens, 26,100 were other EU citizens, and 4,800 were UK citizens. The remaining 81,100 immigrants were citizens of other countries including almost 42,000 Ukrainians. More than half of the immigrants were in the 25–44 age group. Nonetheless, people were also continuing to leave Ireland, so that emigration had not totally ceased, despite popular belief. Over 64,000 people departed the Irish state in the twelve months to April 2023, compared with 56,100 in the same period of 2022, one of the highest figures of recent years.

As the workers at Mary Banotti's nursing home attest, immigrants are filling important positions of employment in Irish society, their labour and skills in high demand, especially in the area of eldercare. With a population of over 5 million based on CSO estimates for April 2023, of these some 803,300 were aged sixty-five and older, an increase of 23.6 per cent since 2017.

Mary Banotti's profile highlights the theme of ageing in Ireland at the start of the twenty-first century and its complications. According to the CSO, the number of people aged sixty-five and over is estimated to have risen by over 40 per cent between 2013 and 2023 and is expected to double again to 1.6 million by 2051.[4] Therefore, in terms of demographics, there is a bulge in the population, and it's at the upper end of the age scale. As life expectancy improves with greater access to healthcare and healthier lifestyles, Irish people are living longer in far greater numbers than at any other time, which means older people will continue to be active and part of Irish society. Unlike in the past, when the religious orders often took care of the elderly in nursing homes, a combination of private and public supply of residences now meets the need, with workers largely drawn from Ireland's new immigrant population. Witnessing Mary Banotti, someone who dedicated her life to public service, appear comfortable and secure in living quarters in Fern Dean seems only right, and no doubt what she calls the 'fair whack' of money required to pay for it comes from her MEP's pension.

With a dramatic increase in Ireland's ageing population there is a major shortage of suitable housing for older people. Restrictions on the state's capacity to invest during the years of austerity after the 2008 economic crash resulted in a severe lack of housing, including specialist housing for the elderly. According to the ESRI, most long-term residential centres (LTRC) are now privately owned by large investors.[5] With the number of elderly people in Ireland increasing and their life expectancy rates improved, it appears that these investors see nursing homes as a profit-making business rather than centres of care. Of course, the state has a role in terms of ensuring standards at nursing homes. In addition, in 2009 the state introduced the Fair Deal system to ensure that families could ensure long-term care for ageing parents by using the family home as collateral against the costs of nursing home care, with the property sold once the person died. It has been extremely popular with families. However, differing experiences between those using Fair Deal to pay for care at private and public homes have been reported by the ESRI.

There has never been such demand for nursing homes. Unlike the historical past, when extended family members cared for ageing relatives, this is no longer a feasible proposition for many Irish families because of the need for two incomes to pay for a mortgage.

During the height of the COVID pandemic, many smaller nursing homes were put under enormous pressure because of staff shortages that caused a cascade of challenges, but the government provided support via the Temporary State Assistance Programme. Nonetheless, many smaller nursing homes across the country closed. Therefore, the supply of nursing homes is now largely the business of bigger operators, not family-owned businesses. Mary's nursing home, Fern Dean, is owned by the Virtue Group, an Irish operation, though *The Irish Times* reported on 3 November 2021 that the French investment firm Emera bought a 70 per cent stake in the company.[6] In addition to Fern Dean, the Virtue Group had three other nursing homes in Ireland in 2021 and was seeking to expand its operations further on the island. Care of Ireland's elderly has become big business.

> This place [the nursing home] was Carmencita Hederman's family home. She was a lord mayor of Dublin. Someone is paying a fair whack [of money] for them [residents] to be here.

During COVID, the elders, those over seventy, were asked by the Irish government to 'cocoon', to isolate themselves in their homes, in order not to be infected with the virus. The impact on older people was to compound their sense of loneliness. Various media carried heartbreaking photos of family members with their palmed hands on the windowpanes, seeking some sense of connection with their elderly relatives. When people died during COVID, including elderly relatives, families were not allowed to attend the funerals.

Possibly as a result of that 'cocoon' experience, older people are even more connected to community since the pandemic, based on some interesting CSO data. With elders living longer, healthier lives in Ireland, they are also more active in society. In 2022, some 58 per cent of those aged seventy-five and over found it very easy to get practical help from neighbours, compared with 40 per cent of those aged from twenty-five to thirty-four. In addition, between 2012 and 2022, the number of people aged seventy and over holding a full driving licence rose by almost 80 per cent, which also suggests that the cohort remains engaged with family and community, not isolated in their homes.

Mary Banotti was a feminist campaigner and politician, dedicated to public service. Her training as a nurse afforded her a profession much in demand that enabled her to travel to many parts of the world. Her travels and her short-lived marriage informed her advocacy work back in Ireland and her political contributions as an MEP in Europe.

Like her grand-uncle, the revolutionary Michael Collins, Mary immersed herself in movements for change to make Ireland a better place, a kinder, more equal society. As a feminist she campaigned with other women leaders on issues long hidden from public view – domestic violence against women and alcohol addiction. Her advocacy had real impact, its benefits accruing to women and families across Ireland. At European Union level, where she served in the European Parliament for twenty years, she focused on environmental policy at committee level, in addition to work on youth, culture, consumer protection and public health. Central to all her contributions and concerns was the welfare of women, informed by her experiences in what was then termed 'the developing world' and her insights as a lone parent living in Ireland from the 1970s. She died in 2024.

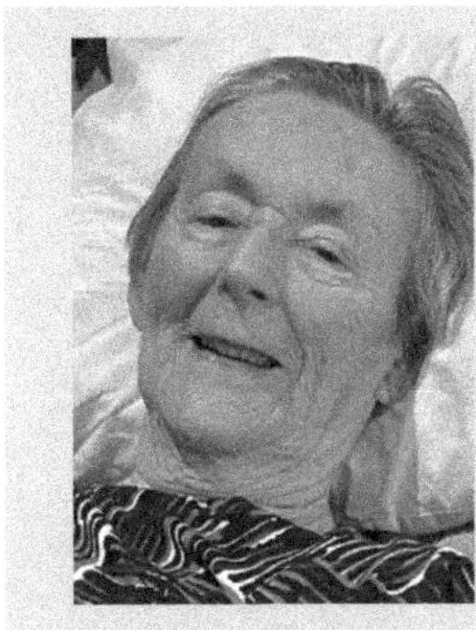

Mary Banotti, 2023
PHOTO BY THE AUTHOR

CONCLUSION

All the women profiled in the previous chapters lived on the island of Ireland during the three decades under consideration in this book, 1993–2023. None of them lived abroad during those years, though many travelled abroad for work or leisure. They were active participants in a society to which they contributed through their labour, and their lives were also shaped by that society over three decades. Six of the seven women profiled lived in the Republic; one was based in Belfast, Northern Ireland.

In this chapter I want to focus on some of the key themes that emerged in each woman's profile, remembering that I crafted the chapter drawing on the information from two interviews conducted over thirty years apart. In that sense, a woman speaks from the point of view of a younger and a more mature self and context, a distinction I've highlighted when necessary. While I recognise that each woman's profile represents a unique perspective and set of circumstances particular to an individual, some key themes emerged that I revisit here in the conclusion. In addition, I explore the larger themes that emerged across the narratives of these seven women's lives, lives lived in various parts of Ireland.

Born into rural poverty in Tipperary, Margaret Galvin's drive to write and her desire to teach others to write from their own experience is informed by those origins. Her creative writing output is imbued with empathy, an understanding of people's dignity in the face of deprivation and forced emigration to England, where all her siblings went, with minimal education. That perspective guided her work as the first woman editor of *Ireland's Own*, a weekly magazine aimed at rural people and members of Ireland's diaspora. When her son's serious health needs were identified, she gave up this coveted job in order to care for him, and 'cried every day for a month'. She understands that country people's needs can be different to those of city dwellers, that the digital connectivity offered by the internet in a modern era can amplify issues like loneliness and isolation. A curse and a blessing, these same technological advances enabled a middle-aged Margaret to earn advanced degrees from her home in Wexford. Resident there for much of her adult life, her primary concern has been supporting her adult son whose neurodiversity challenges require that she and her husband parent for life.

The Rev. Dr Nóirín Ní Riain has had a long and complex relationship with the Catholic Church. On the one hand, she benefited from the shared experience of sacred singing with the monks at Glenstal Abbey in County Limerick, where she lived with her former, late husband and their children, while realising that as a woman she could never become a priest within the Catholic Church. Women remain excluded from that level of engagement. The litany of scandals concerning the abuse of women and children in the care of the Catholic Church over many decades in Ireland has led to its near collapse and eroded its moral authority in the country. Nonetheless, after completing a PhD in theology in middle age, Nóirín persevered with her 'calling' and was ordained an interfaith minister in 2017. She now serves a local and global congregation yearning for meaning and spiritual direction. In her ministry she draws on Celtic spirituality, Catholic rituals she loves and ancient traditions of many world religions. Her use of the internet as her conduit to expand her reach to a loyal global following has been very successful. The Catholic institution she revered prohibited her from becoming a priest, so she chose her own path to realise her desire, reaching thousands of followers from her small home 'Imeall/Edge' in Murroe, County Limerick, just beside Glenstal Abbey.

It was a Catholic nun who recognised and encouraged a young Garry Hynes to realise her directorial talents, developed further during her time attending University College Galway where she co-founded Druid Theatre. Later, as the first woman director of Ireland's national theatre, the Abbey, she realised that not everyone appreciated her approach, and she left to lead Druid, again. Throughout her life she has remained steadfast in her vision of what is required to deliver world-class theatre – encouraging audiences to see anew humanity and its vagaries through her interpretation of dramatic works. An internationally renowned director, she was awarded a Tony in 1998 for her directions of *The Beauty Queen of Leenane* in New York, the first woman to achieve such an honour. Her decision to tour with the DruidO'Casey trilogy in 2023 – three plays created by Seán O'Casey about the period up to and during the emergence of the Irish state – was timely. These dramatic works spur audiences to question twenty-first-century Ireland's economic and social achievements in light of its housing crisis, the aims of the nation state, the functioning of the Republic, and the reality of continuing social class inequalities. The composition of the DruidO'Casey troupe's diverse cast – with two central members of colour – demonstrates Garry's commitment to integration in a diverse Ireland.

Dubliner Olwen Gill has spent most of her adult life living on Ireland's picture-postcard Aran island Inis Mór, a place she visited each summer as a child when there was no running water or electricity available on the island. This stunning landscape of stone and sparse soil is one of the country's most iconic tourist destinations. It is home to several ancient sites like Dún Aengus, thousands of years old, where Olwen now works as a tour guide during the summer months. In the relatively short twelve-week tourist season, over the past three decades she has done what she needs to do to provide for her family, a family she and her husband Michael reared through the Irish language. From running a B&B, to a spell as a fitness instructor, to substitute teaching – she has taken it all in her stride, always engaged with community organisations working collaboratively to protect the island's uniqueness. The internet has enabled Olwen to study from afar, to earn degrees in biodiversity, learning that has informed her community work. Alert to the uniqueness of Inis Mór, she is nonetheless frustrated by the lack of family homes – much of the housing is designated for tourism – and the strict planning regulations that exclude her adult children from returning to the island to rear their families in a Gaeltacht/Irish-speaking area and thereby replenishing the island's Irish-speaking community.

'Peace comes dropping slow', so W.B. Yeats reminds us, and that was the case in terms of the war in Northern Ireland, a place where bombs going off on the streets of Belfast used to be a regular occurrence in the life of a young Ruth Mellish. That was before the Good Friday/Belfast Agreement peace process of 1998. Raised Presbyterian, Ruth has lived through Northern Ireland's war and now its peace, finding her feet at university, a place where she developed her feminist analysis for understanding the society of which she was a part. While the violence on the streets of Belfast is no more, Ruth is concerned about violence against women in the new public space of the internet and on social media platforms. An educator, she feels it is her duty to highlight her concerns about women's safety to her charges, who are part of the digital generation, including the hazy direction of applied artificial intelligence (AI) and its consequences for society. As a middle-aged woman, she's learned first-hand the threat of male violence towards women, especially women in any position of authority. She was stalked by a man for over a year. Traumatised by the experience, there is no trace of Ruth on social media now, no links to her on any public work-related sites. She monitors all internet-based interactions and never posts a photograph of herself online anymore. Violence against women has always been an issue on the island of Ireland. From Ruth's experience, we realise that war can mutate from the real to digital public spaces, with dire consequences, especially for women.

Patricia Hamilton speaks with great affection for the place where she grew up in Sligo – a council house by a river in a beautiful location. Her parents encouraged all their children to avail of education, because of their own limited experience of formal education. Patricia was brilliant, but she learned early on to hide her light – the nuns' message was to be humble, modest, even quiet. She found her niche in the law, working as an advocate, a solicitor. Married to Tom, she wanted to continue her career while raising five children. When Sheryl Sandberg, the former high-flyer at Facebook, advised career women with children to just 'lean in', it seemed like a red rag to a bull for Patricia who had been leaning in and out for decades. Lack of sufficient state childcare scaffolding in support of working mothers was a major challenge. As a result, the family moved from rural Clare into Galway city. As one of only two siblings from her original family to remain working in Ireland, she also took on the responsibility for the health and well-being of her ageing mother in Sligo, until the family found a suitable care home in Dublin. These multiple care responsibilities took their toll on Patricia physically, mentally and emotionally, and she decided to retire early at age sixty.

As the grand-niece of the revolutionary Michael Collins, Mary Banotti's entry into Fine Gael party politics should have been easy, because of this pedigree. However, her status as a lone parent was an impenetrable barrier to her selection by the party to represent them in national politics at that time. An unashamed feminist dedicated to advancing the rights of women in Ireland, she helped to establish its first refuge for women seeking protection from domestic violence. At European level, Mary represented the Dublin constituency in the European Parliament for twenty years. There, her focus was on environmental issues – advocacy well before its time – and on European policy relating to youth, culture and the abduction of children. Despite the challenges she faced in her early political career, she consistently encouraged women from all walks of life and from all political parties to 'put their hat into the [political] ring'. Fern Dean nursing home in Dublin, where she spent her final years, seemed a suitably comfortable place for this dedicated public servant. Her residence reflected a twenty-first-century response to eldercare demand in Dublin –

a Georgian mansion converted into a beautiful, modern facility, staffed by carers from Eastern Europe, India, the Philippines. Her daughter, Tania, continues the family's tradition of public service in her role as director of Creative Ireland. Mary died in 2024, just as this book was being concluded. Her death is the only reference to any event post-2023.

If these are the issues particular to each woman profiled in the book, what are the issues that appear in common to many, if not all? Immigration is a topic that each woman spoke about in the second interview conducted in 2023, a reflection of the fact that by then one in five people on the island was born elsewhere, with the upsurge in numbers evident from the 2000s onwards. The extent of the change in such a short period of time in any society from about 1 per cent immigration in 1993 to about 20 per cent in 2023 is dramatic, so it's not surprising that the women here witnessed its emergence as a major change in Ireland's social landscape. In general, immigration was not necessarily perceived as a challenge by the women in this book, rather a new phenomenon that needed to be managed. In fact, the benefit of immigrants' contribution to the Irish workforce was evident in Mary Banotti's case. Her care during her residency in a nursing home was largely in the hands of immigrants. Margaret Galvin spoke about her experience of volunteering as an English-language tutor with IPAs (international protection applicants) in Wexford. She was critical of the government's preparation and communication with communities prior to the arrival of immigrants, especially in places with limited resources in education and health. She suggests that 'cultural competence works both ways', explaining that facilitated integration also includes education – for the native population on migrants' places of origin, and for migrants on cultural norms in Ireland, for example learning basic greetings, acknowledging women's presence in company and other acceptable social mores that build goodwill in communities. Patricia Hamilton talks about the different languages she hears rising from the people walking along the Galway beach where she swims daily – Ireland's diversity in full view in the great outdoors, without any problems arising, from her point of view. Even on Olwen Gill's home place, Inis Mór, immigrant workers are crucial to the functioning of its tourism industry. Therefore, there is a general acknowledgement that immigrant workers are the backbone of Ireland's care and services sectors in Ireland.

Another major social issue in Ireland in 2023 is housing. Garry Hynes explains that the housing crisis was a direct result of the government's decision to bail out the 'bankers' in 2008, with dire consequences for people seeking to rent and own homes since that time. In 2023, almost 13,000 people are homeless in the Republic, including almost 4,000 children. In Olwen Gill's case, the Irish government's inadequate response to housing need and convoluted planning policy is a hindrance to her adult children's desire to return to Inis Mór and raise their children through Irish in the Gaeltacht. With one government department advocating support of Gaeltacht communities and another restricting families from returning to the place of their birth because of planning regulations, there is clearly a need for reform. All of Patricia Hamilton's adult children were working for income, having attended college, but all were still renting, unable to afford a mortgage.

Education is the third theme that emerged as important across all seven women's lives. In her middle years, Margaret Galvin, based in Wexford, availed of a hybrid model of education to achieve a basic and advanced degree, excelling in both to such an extent that she was named student of the year of her graduating class. Mary Banotti, who first trained as a nurse in the 1960s in England, re-trained as a social worker while living abroad. Patricia Hamilton first trained as a teacher and then as a solicitor. Despite her isolation on Inis Mór, Olwen Gill studied for and graduated with her advanced degree, an experience facilitated by new technology and the internet. Ruth Mellish went where her mother never did – to university – where she thrived. Ruth's mother encouraged her as did Patricia's mother and father, all of whom had limited formal education. Nóirín Ní Riain graduated with a PhD in middle age – no small feat. All of the women profiled in this book were more educated than their mothers, reflecting the national trend of increasing numbers of women – and now more women than men – attending and graduating from universities in Ireland. However, despite that trend, only relatively small numbers of women are in leadership positions in the professions, in business and in politics – places where powerful decision-making in relation to society takes place.

The 2023 European Union Gender Equality Index ranks Ireland at ninth place of its twenty-seven member states, a reflection of the fact that Irish women spend much more time on care and domestic work than Irish men. Therefore, after three decades of progress, equality remains a major challenge in Irish society. Even though there are more women graduating from universities than men, they remain locked out of the higher-end jobs because of their need to juggle childcare and domestic work with a career, as was the case with Patricia Hamilton. In twenty-first-century Ireland, government programmes in support of childcare have not met demand, and lack of suitable childcare continues to limit women's progression in work and education. Women are still concentrated in lower-paid work and are largely absent from positions at the top of organisations, business and politics because society has not prioritised state provision of free childcare to all.

In fact, in 2023, women are woefully underrepresented in politics at all levels, and more alarmingly, are subject to frightening levels of violence and misogyny in public and private spaces in Ireland. Socialisation in Ireland – in families and in education – appears to be recreating traditional gender roles, despite women's engagement with the labour market, with education and so forth. As a result, Irish men seem to expect women to take on responsibility for the domestic sphere and the care of children – in addition to their paid work. This phenomenon is not unique to Ireland, but nonetheless there is clearly work to be done in the education system to address these gender expectations if women are ever to achieve their full potential in Irish society.

In the thirty years covered in this book, 1993–2023, Irish women attained more rights than their mothers and grandmothers, rights hard won through advocacy and campaigns organised by women's groups, community and advocacy groups building coalitions with like-minded citizens to push for change. Legislative changes are a reality in several crucial areas impacting the lives of women, but it is the mainstreaming of change – ensuring that measures brought into law are working on the ground – that can be challenging. The women in this book lived lives in the context of major social change. Their pragmatic reading of the landscape of change helped to determine what was possible to improve their lives and what might pose a challenge. In that sense, they were contributors to and beneficiaries of social change processes.

Access to contraception to ensure reproductive control is now a reality, enabling choices over when and how many children a woman bears, if she wishes to, in her lifetime. Abortion is legal, available in theory since 2018, though problems exist in terms of access nationally. Since 1996, women have the right to divorce, another crucial piece of legislation facilitating choice and direction in a woman's life. Lesbians can choose to marry their partners since 2015, if they wish to do so, and enjoy the rights and privileges of married heterosexual couples. These three vital pieces of legislative change in particular – divorce, marriage equality and abortion – have only been achieved in relatively recent years, albeit through referenda in each case, which means citizens debated the issues and voted in relation to these constitutional changes. However, it's been a long road from the advocacy of second-wave feminism in the 1970s to these recent successful campaigns for social change.

In the thirty years that form the focus of this book, 1993–2023, the position of women in Irish society has improved significantly according to several indices like life expectancy, quality of life, and opportunity. According to WHO data, life expectancy was 84.4 years for women in 2020, up from 75 years in the 1990s. In fact, Ireland is ranked within the top twenty countries in the world in terms of life expectancy and is the best in Europe. There's full employment, a thriving economy with massive surpluses and significant inward migration which means that migrants will contribute to Ireland's labour force and tax base, an important consideration given its ageing population. There are challenges in relation to a chronic housing shortage, homelessness, healthcare, the digital world and AI. Advocacy in relation to violence against women has had an impact on government policy and practice and there are signs of real progress. In 2022, the government published a zero tolerance plan on domestic, sexual and gender-based violence (DSGBV) and established a national DSGBV agency in 2023.[1] Coercive control became illegal in 2019, and in 2021 Ireland adopted 'Coco's Law', the criminalisation of image-based sexual abuse, in response to women's experience of harassment or abuse on social media. In 2023, a directive on gender-based violence is progressing through the EU, spearheaded by Frances Fitzgerald, MEP. These developments are important in the context of the issues raised in relation to women's safety in public and private spaces as outlined in Ruth Mellish's narrative in Chapter 6.

The number of women engaged in Irish politics remains an issue, despite the introduction of gender-based quotas in the 2016 general election. In 2021, Minister for Justice Helen McEntee became the first member of cabinet to take maternity leave, which was the catalyst for a renewed public discussion on the link between adequate childcare support and Irish women's engagement in politics at all levels. In 2022, contraceptives were made free to all seventeen- to twenty-five-year-olds in Ireland, ensuring reproductive control for younger women.

Following Mary Robinson's election as the first woman president of Ireland, women's groups across the country demonstrated renewed energy and drive to come together, to build connections in common cause, to work collectively on key issues, and to campaign and advocate for change to make Ireland a more just, fair and equal country. Supported by a national body, the National Women's Council of Ireland (NWCI), in addition to community development and EU programmes, and philanthropic bodies throughout the 1990s, Irish women demonstrated a growing confidence in their power and capacity to shape Irish society through their collective efforts at community, regional, national and EU levels. The extent and nature of that capacity-building of the women's sector – which resulted in women's greater participation in the workforce and in policy fora – has not been replicated since the 1990s. In 2000, with the Millenium Project, an initiative facilitated by the NWCI, women's groups throughout the island were supported to identify the key issues impacting their lives, trained in community-based research methods such as needs analysis, and they learned how to prepare policy position papers and were supported to submit them to various policy fora. Taken together, these spokes in the wheel of change represented a momentum for women and they had impact.

Crucial to this enhanced engagement with society was women's growing economic power. Irish women's participation in the labour force has grown in the thirty years under review, all evident in the narratives in this book, even after the 2008 global economic crash. However, in general, Irish women's continued concentration in the mid- to lower-level positions of work rather than in the upper echelons of employment sectors demonstrates a limited success. Conversely, given the work practices expected of leaders in high-level positions, women may decide that these jobs come at too high a cost – in terms of personal and family life – and not seek them. Similarly, women's continued underrepresentation in politics, despite a commitment to gender quotas by political parties, continues to be a challenge. The strategies of the past – to build the capacity of the women's sector – seem less applicable in the current context since it appears that there is little consensus in relation to key women's issues in Irish society, in addition to robust debates on what constitutes the category 'woman'.

Nonetheless, the women's narratives in this book – Margaret Galvin, Nóirín Ní Riain, Garry Hynes, Olwen Gill, Ruth Mellish, Patricia Hamilton and Mary Banotti – women from different walks of life, with varied experiences of social change over thirty years, demonstrate a capacity to creatively respond to the changing social context, to seek solutions to challenges when necessary, and to harness support when it's needed. What their lives tell us is that despite the social conditions they encountered at various points in their lives, the lack of opportunities or support, through their actions they made the conditions of their lives work for them. Their narratives provide evidence of individual flexibility and resilience in a context of enormous social change, including their capacity to shift the landscape to ensure that they reach their potential.

Classicist Mary Beard in her book *Women and Power* reminds us that the silencing of women's voices in public was the expected norm for centuries, with only two exceptions in the classical world – women were allowed to speak as victims and martyrs, or in defence of their homes and children.[2] In a twenty-first-century context, where the new public space is virtual, digital, not real, we need to be attuned to what Beard calls 'the processes and prejudices that make us not listen' to women. 'The personal is political', as feminism reminds us, and indeed the narratives in this book are deeply personal and political, and worthy of our attention. We have much to learn from these accounts of Irish women's lives. Annie G. Rogers, *Harvard Project on Women's Psychology and Girls' Development*, reminds us that by listening to women's narratives we acknowledge their courage in the thirteenth-century definition of the word: 'to speak one's mind by telling all one's heart'. Therefore, these accounts of Irish women's lives from 1993 to 2023 are simply courageous and inspirational.

NOTES

[All URL links were accessible at time of publication]

Foreword

1. Gráinne Healy is a feminist activist, researcher and author, was editor at Attic Press, chairwoman of the National Women's Council of Ireland, chair of Marriage Equality, vice-president of the European Women's Lobby and president of the EU's Observatory on Violence Against Women. www.grainnehealy.ie.

Introduction

1. The *Harvard Project on Women's Psychology and Girls' Development* was led by Professor Carol Gilligan in the 1990s, and involved a number of leading researchers, including Annie G. Rogers. Its research focused on girls' development in adolescence, tracing how girls' voices become less confident and more uncertain as they learn the social world's expectations of them as women.

2. President Mary Robinson's inauguration, 3 December 1990, https://www.youtube.com/watch?v=_hD_XHnobV0.

3. RTÉ Archives, *The Age of Equality?*, 10 November 1990, https://www.rte.ie/archives/2020/1023/1173435-male-chauvinism.

4. See www.ocainternational.com for a list of research completed during these years.

5. UK philanthropic bodies active in the Irish social change context in the 1990s included the Joseph Rowntree Charitable Trust and The Allen Lane Foundation. Later, The Atlantic Philanthropies, established by Irish-American Chuck Feeney, was a limited-life foundation that was a major contributor to social change processes (closed 2018). The One Foundation (2004–14), founded by Deirdre Mortell and Ryanair's Declan Ryan, was the first home-grown limited-life, Irish philanthropic organisation. The Community Foundation Ireland began its work in 2000 and is still active.

Chapter 1: Context – The Changing Role of Women in Irish Society, 1993–2023

1. P. Daly, *The Evolution of Irish Household Wealth Inequality Since 2013: Insights from new distributional wealth accounts* (Dublin: Central Bank, 2022).

2. Central Statistics Office (CSO). Data drawn from the CSO throughout the book can be accessed at www.cso.ie.

3. OECD, 'Ireland Economic Snapshot', https://www.oecd.org/en/topics/sub-issues/economic-surveys/ireland-economic-snapshot.html.

4. The New Opportunities for Women (NOW) programme was established in December 1990 by the European Commission. Its first rollout was from 1991 to '95. The second iteration was from 1995 to '99. In Ireland, the programme was managed by the National Women's Council of Ireland (NWCI). For more on the NOW programme in Ireland, see www.ocainternational.com.

5. In her memoir, Sinéad recalls: 'There was so much pain, after all, involved with being a pariah for decades after SNL'. S. O'Connor, *Rememberings* (New York: HarperCollins, 2021).

6. *Report of the Commission to Inquire into Child Abuse* (Ryan Report) (2009), https://www.gov.ie/en/publication/3c76d0-the-report-of-the-commission-to-inquire-into-child-abuse-the-ryan-re.

7. Important source material on Magdalene laundries can be found at: https://jfmresearch.com/home/preserving-magdalene-history/about-the-magdalene-laundries.

8. The pioneering research of media expert Dr Joan Donovan, former research director at Harvard Kennedy School's Shorenstein Center for Media, Politics and Public Policy, is crucial to our understanding of this strategy. In 2021, in her statement to the US Senate Committee on the Judiciary Subcommittee on Privacy, Technology, and the Law, entitled 'Algorithms and Amplification: How social media platforms' design choices shape our discourse and our minds' (27 April 2021), she reported that the social media companies' business model was based on increasing engagement metrics and active users and thereby increasing revenue: 'Increasing engagement meant delivering more novel and outrageous content, which is why false news, harassment, and defamation thrive on social media.' https://www.judiciary.senate.gov/imo/media/doc/Donovan%20Testimony%20(updated).pdf.

Chapter 2: Margaret Galvin

Broadcasts

The following essays have been broadcast on *Sunday Miscellany*, RTÉ Radio 1, https://www.rte.ie/radio/radio1/sunday-miscellany:

'Twill Shorten the Winter for Us', 23 October 2021

'The Turkey Pluckers' Concert', 12 December 2021

'Keep Young and Beautiful', 13 February 2022

'Johnny Boyle's Lessons', 27 February 2022

'The Day I Invented the Washing Machine', 27 March 2022

'Easter Heirlooms', 17 April 2022

'The Harm of the Year Go with It', 12 June 2022

'Johnny Ledger's Legacy', 21 August 2022

'Tackling the Road', 2 October 2022

'Rude Good Health', 15 January 2023

'Parcels from London', 23 January 2023

'I'd Love a Babycham', 5 March 2023

'A Gift from the Family', 23 December 2023

The following poems have been broadcast on *Sunday Miscellany*:

'Under the Bridges of Paris', 19 February 2022

'Uncle Billy's Fortune', 3 April 2022

'My Mother Hoped for the Best', 9 October 2022

'Mourning at Blondie', 19 February 2023

The following reflection has been broadcast on *A Word in Edgeways*, RTÉ Radio 1, https://www.rte.ie/radio/radio1/edgeways:

'The Full Irish', 14 December 2023

Poetry Collections by Margaret Galvin

Miresuck and Slaver (London: Tuba Press, 1989)

Habitual Keeper (London: Tuba Press, 1993)

The Waiting Room (Tralee: Doghouse, 2005)

The Wishbone (Wexford: Wexford County Council Library Service, 2007)

The Wardrobe Mistress (Belfast: Lapwing, 2009)

The Scattering Lawns (Belfast: Lapwing, 2013)

The Finer Points (Cahir: Cahir Social and Historical Society, 2019)

Our House, Delirious (Limerick: Revival Press, 2023)

Collections compiled and edited by Margaret Galvin

Around Each Bend: Poetry and prose by Tipperary writers (Nenagh: Tipperary County Council Arts Office, 2021)

Bridging the Distance: A focus on four Tipperary writers (Nenagh: Tipperary County Council Arts Office (a Bealtaine project), 2022)

Chapter 3: Nóirín Ní Riain

1. M. Condren, *The Serpent and the Goddess: Women, religion and power in Celtic Ireland* (San Francisco: Harpers, 1989), p. 16.

2. S. Ó Duinn, *The Rites of Brigid: Goddess and saint* (Dublin: Columba Press, 2005).

3. On the US radio programme *NPR Morning Edition*, on 26 August 2015 Maeve Lewis said that 'the most damaging thing to the Catholic Church here was not the fact that priests actually abused children. It was the wide-scale cover-ups that went on at very senior levels. That's what people find unforgivable.'

4. See Nóirín's website: www.noirin.love.

5. With her two sons, Eoin and Mícheál, Nóirín facilitates annual pilgrimages to sacred spaces in Ireland: www.turasdanam.com.

Chapter 4: Garry Hynes

1. https://www.druid.ie/productions/druidocasey/the-trilogy.

2. 'In the Fires of Rebellion and War', Druid Theatre's Garry Hynes in conversation with Fintan O'Toole, Galway International Arts Festival, July 2023, https://www.youtube.com/watch?v=8IgLudAN9pU.

3. P. Woodworth, 'Hynes to Break with Abbey because of Rift with Board', *Irish Times*, 7 April 1993.

4. L. Collins-Hughes, 'Garry Hynes Brings Seán O'Casey's Trilogy to Life', *New York Times*, 4 October 2023.

Chapter 5: Olwen Gill

1. Central Statistics Office, 'Census 2022, Results Profile 8, The Irish Language and Education', https://www.cso.ie/en/csolatestnews/pressreleases/2023pressreleases/pressstatementcensus2022resultsprofile8-theirishlanguageandeducation.

2. A. Healy, 'Salmon Farm Plan Caught on Hook of Controversy', *Irish Times*, 4 March 2013.

Chapter 6: Ruth Mellish

1. Department of Foreign Affairs, Ireland, 'About the Good Friday Agreement', https://www.ireland.ie/en/dfa/role-policies/northern-ireland/about-the-good-friday-agreement.

2. P. Sehgal, 'How the Writer and Critic Jacqueline Rose Puts the World on the Couch', *The New Yorker*, 14 August 2023.

Chapter 7: Patricia Hamilton

1. A.R. Hochschild, *So, How's the Family? And other essays* (San Francisco: University of California Press, 2013).

2. S. Sandberg, *Lean In: Women, work, and the will to lead* (New York: Alfred A. Knopf, 2013).

3. National Women's Council of Ireland, budget submission on childcare, 5 September 2023, https://www.nwci.ie/learn/article/call_to_deliver_public_childcare_as_part_of_budget_2024; Citizens Information, 'Your Childcare Options, https://www.citizensinformation.ie/en/education/pre-school-education-and-childcare/your-childcare-options.

4. Hochschild, *So, How's the Family*.

Chapter 8: Mary Banotti

1. Dictionary of Irish Biography, https://www.dib.ie/biography/fennell-nuala-a9736.

2. European Commission Guide on EU Sources and Information, https://ec-europa-eu.libguides.com/EU_sources.

3. M. Banotti, *There's Something About Mary: Conversations with Irish women politicians* (Dublin: Currach Press, 2008).

4. https://www.cso.ie/en/releasesandpublications/hubs/p-opi/olderpersonsinformationhub/ageingpopulation.

5. B. Walsh, *Long-Term Residential Care in Ireland* (Dublin: ESRI, 2023).

6. F. Redden, 'Foxrock Nursing Home Gears up for Expansion', *Irish Times*, 3 November 2021.

Conclusion

1. https://www.gov.ie/en/department-of-justice/press-releases/government-approves-publication-of-legislation-to-establish-new-domestic-sexual-and-gender-based-violence-agency (18 September 2023).

2. M. Beard, *Women & Power: A manifesto* (London: Profile Books, 2017).

BIBLIOGRAPHY

Banotti, M., *There's Something About Mary: Conversations with Irish women politicians* (Dublin: Currach Press, 2008)

Beard, M., *Women & Power: A manifesto* (London: Profile Books, 2017)

Central Statistics Office, *Census of Population Report* (Dublin: CSO, 2022)

———, *Principal Economic Status, 1986–2022* (Dublin: CSO, 2022)

———, *Economic Indicators: Ireland and the EU at 50* (Dublin: CSO, 2023)

———, *Labour Market Economy: Ireland and the EU at 50* (Dublin: CSO, 2023)

———, *Population and Migration Estimates* (Dublin: CSO, 2023)

Condren, M., *The Serpent and the Goddess: Women, religion and power in Celtic Ireland* (San Francisco: Harpers, 1989)

Coolahan, J., 'Higher Education in Ireland: Country background report', in *Higher Education in Ireland*, OECD review of national policies and education services (Paris: OECD, 2014)

Daly, P., *The Evolution of Irish Household Wealth Inequality Since 2013: Insights from new distributional wealth accounts* (Dublin: Central Bank, 2022)

Donovan, J. et al., *Meme Wars: The untold story of the online battles upending democracy in America* (New York: Bloomsbury, 2022)

Ferriter, D., *The Transformation of Ireland 1900–2000* (London: Profile, 2004)

———, *Occasions of Sin: Sex and society in modern Ireland* (London: Profile, 2009)

Hartford, J., *The Opening of University Education to Women in Ireland* (Dublin: Irish Academic Press, 2008)

Hochschild, A.R., *So, How's the Family? And other essays* (San Francisco: University of California Press, 2013)

Holland, M., *How Far We Have Travelled: Selected columns from* The Irish Times (Dublin: Townhouse, 2004)

Inglis, T., 'A Religious Frenzy', in M. Peillon and E. Slater (eds), *Encounters with Modern Ireland* (Dublin: Institute of Public Administration, 1998)

Kirby, P., *The Celtic Tiger in Distress: Growth with inequality in Ireland* (Basingstoke: Palgrave, 2002)

Laurence, J. et al., *The Changing Social and Political Attitudes in Ireland and Northern Ireland* (Dublin: ESRI, 2023)

Lynch, K., *Equality in Education* (Dublin: Gill & Macmillan, 1999)

McAleese, M., *Here's the Story: A memoir* (Milton Keynes: Penguin Random House, 2020)

McCafferty, N., *The Best of Nell: A selection of writings over fourteen years* (Cork: Cork University Press/Attic, 1984)

Migrant Rights Centre Ireland, *Realising Integration: Creating the conditions for economic, social, political and cultural inclusion of migrant workers and their families in Ireland* (Dublin: MRCI, 2006)

Ní Riain, N., *Listen with the Ear of the Heart: An autobiography* (Dublin: Veritas, 2009)

O'Carroll, Í., *Models for Movers: Irish women's emigration to America* (Dublin/Cork: Attic/Cork University Press, 1990/2015)

———, *Daring Voices: The One Foundation's support of work in the areas of immigrant rights, children's rights and youth mental health in Ireland* (2013), https://www.advocacyinitiative.ie/resource/daring-voices-evaluation-one-foundations-advocacy-work

———, 'Across the Pond: Connections to marriage equality', in G. Healy and O. Howard (eds), *Crossing the Threshold: The story of the marriage equality movement* (Dublin: Merrion Press, 2017)

———, *Irish Transatlantics, 1980–2015* (Cork: Cork University Press/Attic, 2018)

O'Carroll, Í. and E. Collins (eds), *Lesbian and Gay Visions of Ireland: Towards the twenty-first century* (London: Cassells, 1995)

O'Cleary, C., *The Billionaire Who Wasn't: How Chuck Feeney secretly made and gave away a fortune* (New York: Public Affairs, 2007)

O'Connor, S., *Rememberings* (New York: HarperCollins, 2021)

Ó Duinn, S., *The Rites of Brigid: Goddess and saint* (Dublin: Columba Press, 2005)

O'Rourke, M., *Just Mary: A memoir* (Dublin: Gill & Macmillan, 2012)

Robinson, M., *Everybody Matters: My life giving voice* (New York: Walker & Company, 2002)

Ruhs, M. and E. Quinn, *Ireland: From rapid immigration to recession*, Migration Policy Institute, 2009, https://www.migrationpolicy.org/article/ireland-rapid-immigration-recession

Sandberg, S., *Lean In: Women, work, and the will to lead* (New York: Alfred A. Knopf, 2013)

Walsh, B., *Long-Term Residential Care in Ireland* (Dublin: ESRI, 2023)

INDEX

Note: Page locators in bold refer to photographs.